A Gift for

_____

Presented by

_____

I Used to Know That

"I've a grand memory for forgetting."

—Robert Louis Stevenson

I Used to Know That

Know That

stuff you forgot from school

Caroline Taggart

Reader's
Digest

The Reader's Digest Association, Inc.
Pleasantville, New York / Montreal

*For Jon and Nic, who are old enough to start forgetting
this sort of stuff; and for Mishak and Camille, who
are just beginning to learn it.*

A READER'S DIGEST BOOK

Copyright © 2009 Michael O'Mara Books Limited

All rights reserved. Unauthorized reproduction, in any manner,
is prohibited.

Reader's Digest is a registered trademark of The Reader's Digest
Association, Inc.

First published in Great Britain in 2008 by Michael O'Mara Books Limited, 9 Lion Yard,
Tremadoc Road, London SW4 7NQ

READER'S DIGEST TRADE PUBLISHING
U.S. Project Editor: Kimberly Casey
Consulting Editor: Sandra Kear
Copy Editor: Barbara Booth
Canadian Project Editor: Pamela Johnson
Canadian Consulting Editor: J. D. Gravenor
Project Production Coordinator: Wayne Morrison
Senior Art Director: George McKeon
Executive Editor: Dolores York
Manufacturing Manager: Elizabeth Dinda
Associate Publisher: Rosanne McManus
President and Publisher: Harold Clarke

Library of Congress Cataloging-in-Publication Data:

Taggart, Caroline.
  I used to know that : stuff you forgot from school / Caroline Taggart.
     p. cm.
  "A Reader's digest book"--T.p. verso.
  "First published in Great Britain in 2008 by Michael O'Mara Books"--T.p.
verso.
  ISBN 978-0-7621-0995-1
  1. Handbooks, vade-mecums, etc. I. Title.
  AG105.T14 2009
  031.02--dc22
                                                              2008033112

The author would like to thank Ana, who wanted me to write this book; Silvia, for making it
happen and for sharing my loathing of *Wuthering Heights*, and the other Ana, for neck-breaking
design. Thanks, also, to everyone who has entered into the spirit of it and made enthusiastic
suggestions, even if I haven't had room to include them all. Special thanks to Bob for vetting the
math and science chapters and pointing out that pi isn't a recurring decimal. I used to know that.

Reader's Digest is committed to both the quality of our products and the service we
provide to our customers. We value your comments, so please feel free to contact us:
The Reader's Digest Association, Inc., Adult Trade Publishing,
Reader's Digest Road, Pleasantville, NY 10570-7000

For more Reader's Digest products and information, visit our website:
www.rd.com (in the United States)
www.readersdigest.ca (in Canada)

Printed in the United States

7 9 10 8 6

CONTENTS

Introduction

When I started to write this book, I realized that I did remember lots of different things, but I didn't always remember those facts completely, or necessarily accurately. I knew, for example, that "The Assyrian came down like a wolf on the fold" was a perfect example of—what—a dactyl or an anapest? I had to look it up. I remembered a bit about sines and cosines but had no idea why they were important. I used to know most of the principal bones in the body. How did that song go? "The head bone's connected to the neck bone, the neck bone's connected to the..." Hmmm. And after years of study, I could not seem to name the dates of important wars or, for that matter, why they were fought (I'm still having some trouble with that).

Geography was especially challenging—just when I thought I knew the capital of Burma, they change everything. Myanmar is tragically all over the news, and I'm left scratching my head in bewilderment as to where it is exactly. There's also a wealth of general information that I thought I knew, like Roman numerals and the Roman equivalent to the Greek gods.

Sometimes I hear a symphony and all I can remember is that it was composed by a man whose last name starts with V...or was it B?

In the course of talking to other people about what I should include in this book, I discovered two things: one, that everybody I spoke to had been to school, and two, that that was pretty much all they had in common. They had all forgotten completely different things. So with every conversation the book seemed to grow longer. One chat with an editor friend sent me rushing to add the active and passive voices to the English chapter. Another friend could recite British poetry verbatim but could not remember if the poem she so eloquently performed was by Keats or Shelley. Yet another friend confessed that she had completely forgotten what a square root was (though I have no idea why she suddenly wanted to know). In the end I had to stop discussing it, or this book would have surpassed the size of *War and Peace*. I also found in the course of researching the things I used to know that I learned more than a few things that I didn't.

All of which is a roundabout way of saying that I hope you, too, will learn something new or find things here that strike a chord, however faintly. Things that make you say, "Oh, yes, I used to know that." Because by the time you read this, I will almost certainly have forgotten most of them again.

ENGLISH

Learning to read and write was just the beginning. After you had mastered that, you had to study how the language worked and, when you started to write your own stories, how to stay focused, develop content, organize material, maintain a consistent voice and style, *and* use proper grammar. If (perish the thought) you had to write poetry as well, there was a whole new set of conventions....

Parts of Speech

This is a way of categorizing words according to the function they perform in a sentence, and there are nine of them:

adjective: a describing word. Some examples include *tall, short, brown,* and *blue*. With one possible exception—*blond/blonde*—adjectives in English (unlike most European languages) are invariable; that is, they don't change according to the number and gender of the thing they are describing.

adverb: a word that describes a verb, an adjective, or another adverb. Adverbs answer such questions as how, when, or where: *She walked aimlessly; light brown hair* (where *light* is an adverb describing the adjective *brown*); *they lived fairly frugally* (where *fairly* is an adverb describing the adverb *frugally*). Most, but by no means all, adverbs in English are formed by adding *-ly* to the adjective.

article: *Merriam-Webster* defines an article as "any small words or affixes…used with nouns to limit or give definiteness to the application." That's not very helpful, is it? It may be easier just to remember that the definite article is *the* and the indefinite articles are *a* and *an*.

conjunction: a joining word. Examples include *and, but, though,* and so on. Conjunctions link two words, phrases, or clauses together: Pride **and** Prejudice *is Jane Austen's most popular book,* **but** *I also love* Sense **and** Sensibility, ***though*** *Marianne can be really annoying.*

interjection: a word to express emotion. For example, *Aha!* or *Alas!*

noun: a naming word. There are three categories:
- Collective nouns describe a group of things. However, they are funny things. There are some genuinely useful ones to describe animals that live in groups—you wouldn't talk about a gaggle of elephants, for example, or a flock of lions. But at some stage in history, someone thought it was useful to give collective names to almost a hundred birds where you might have thought that *group, colony,* or *a whole bunch* would serve the purpose. And there are many variations. If you are talking about a group of ducks, for example, you could say a *badelynge, brace, bunch, dopping, flock, paddling, plump, raft, safe, skein, sord, string,* or *team. A charm of goldfinches, an exaltation of larks,* and *a parliament of owls* are often quoted but rarely used in real life—but once you start Googling for this sort of thing, you also come across *a dopping of goosanders.* (Goosanders? Some people have too much time on their hands.)

- <u>Proper nouns</u> name a person, place, or thing that requires a capital letter, such as *Caroline, Paris,* or the *Smithsonian Institution.*
- <u>Common nouns</u> cover general terms, such as *street, book,* and *photograph.*

preposition: a word that links nouns, pronouns, and phrases and indicates their relationship to the object in a sentence. Prepositions include words such as *beside, through, over, during, at, in, to, on: The boy stood* on *the burning deck; it was Greek* to *me.*

pronoun: a word that stands in the place of a noun. For instance, *Caroline has forgotten a lot of stuff. That is why* she *is writing this book*—where the pronoun *she* in the second sentence takes the place of the proper noun *Caroline* in the first. Other examples include *it, he, her, his, me,* and *they.*

verb: a doing word. A verb indicates the occurrence or performance of an action, or the existence of a state or condition, such as *to be, to do, to run, to happen.* This form of a verb (normally containing the word *to*) is called the **infinitive.** Verbs change their form according to tense, person, and number: *I am, I was, you were, he is, they are.* Verbs can also be in the **active** or **passive voice**—*I bake the bread* is active; *the bread is baked* is passive. English also has three verb moods: the **indicative** makes a simple statement—*I bake the bread*; the **subjunctive** indicates something that is wished or possible—*If I were you, I would bake the bread*; and the **imperative** gives a command—*Bake that bread!*

Phrases and Clauses

Now it is time to take a look at the building blocks of sentences: phrases and clauses. Each depends on the other to express a complete thought, but knowing the difference between them can be quite confusing. Generally, you can rely on the following definitions:

- A **phrase** is a group of words (in a sentence) that does not contain a subject or verb—or either one: *In the afternoon, we went to the store.*

- A **clause** does contain a subject and a verb and may stand alone as a sentence or as part of a sentence (when it is often called a **subordinate clause**): *He loves dogs* but doesn't have one.

Sentences—and each clause of a sentence—can be divided into a **subject** and a **predicate**.

- The **subject** is the noun or noun phrase that the sentence is about, the thing that does the action expressed in the verb.

- The **predicate** is everything else. In sentences involving the verb *to be*, what follows the verb is known as the **complement**, as in *Silence is golden,* where *golden* is the complement of the verb.

- A verb may be **transitive** or **intransitive,** which means it may or may not need a direct object in order to make sense. The **object** is the thing on which the subject performs the action of the verb. In the sentence *He hit the ball*, the object is *ball.*

To see some examples of all this, consider a line from *A Midsummer Night's Dream:*

I know a bank whereon the wild thyme blows.

The main statement or principal clause is *I know a bank.* Not very interesting, but it stands alone as a sentence. *I* is the subject, *know a bank* is the predicate and can be subdivided into the verb *know,* and the object (answering the question What do I know?), is *bank. Know* in this sentence is a transitive verb—it doesn't make much sense without the object.

The subordinate clause is *whereon the wild thyme blows.* The clause has a verb (*blows*) with a subject (*the wild thyme,* which is a noun phrase), but it isn't a sentence. Note, however, that *blows* makes sense on its own—it doesn't need an object, so it is intransitive.

Blow is one of many verbs that can be either transitive or intransitive, depending on context: The wind blows intransitively, but you can blow a horn or blow glass in a transitive way.

Taking a sentence apart to analyze its components is called **parsing**. You may remember drawing a parse tree or **sentence diagram** in elementary school.

Synonyms, Antonyms, and the Like

The suffix *-nym* derives from the Greek for *name,* but in fact, these words are currently used to refer to meaning. So a **synonym** is a word that has the same or similar meaning as another, while an **antonym** has the opposite meaning.

Here are some examples:
- *Spooky, scary, frightening,* and *eerie* are **synonyms,** as are *pale, wan,* and *ashen.*
- *Mean* is an **antonym** of *generous.*

Illogically, a **homonym** is a word that has the same spelling as another, but a different meaning. A **homophone** sounds like another word but doesn't have the same spelling. Confused?

English abounds in homonyms and homophones, which are often completely unrelated in the etymological sense.
- *Eerie* (spooky) is a homophone of *eyrie* (an eagle's nest).
- *Pale* (light in color) is a homonym of *pale* (a fence, as in *beyond the pale*) and a homophone of *pail* (a bucket).
- *Mean* (miserly) is a homonym of *mean* (intend) and a homophone of *mien* (appearance).

All those silly mistakes that spell-checkers fail to detect, such as *there* and *their,* are homophones.

Diphthongs

Diphthongs are complicated things. What most people think of as a diphthong is actually a digraph or ligature, and true diphthongs are often written as a single letter, which makes them less obvious to readers.

Huh?

OK. *Merriam-Webster* defines a diphthong as "a gliding monosyllabic speech sound that starts at or near the articulatory position of one vowel and moves to or toward the position of another."

Try it for yourself and feel the difference when you say *late* and *bat* or *loud* and *catch*. Listen for the glides (*y* or *w*) at the end of the vowel sound.

Diphthongs may be written as a single letter (the *i* in *white* and the *o* in *no*, for example) or as two (*ui* in *fruit*, *ea* in *heat*). Any combination of two letters, whether vowels or consonants that produces a single sound is known as a *digraph,* so that includes not only the *ui* in *fruit* and the *ea* in *heat* but also the *ph* in *photograph* and the *dg* in bridge.

Many North American words that are spelled with a single letter are represented by two letters in their British counterparts. The *ae* written together in the British spelling of *encyclopaedia* or *mediaeval* is, strictly speaking, a ligature, which means that the two letters are joined together as one. This has its origins with medieval scribes who were simply trying to save time and space by combining the two letters on the same block when it was transferred to hot metal type. Modern typesetting doesn't recognize ligatures, so the tendency since the 1950s has been to write the two letters separately or, increasingly, to drop one of them altogether—with the result that, in British English, *encyclopaedia* and *mediaeval* look rather old-fashioned, while in American English *encyclopedia* and *medieval* have become the standard.

Figures of Speech (and other devices for spicing up your writing)

A figure of speech is technically an expression used in a nonliteral (that is, a figurative) way, such as when you say *My lips are sealed.* Obviously, this is not possible unless you have put glue over them. When most people learn ways to expand their writing style, they are often directed to utilize such techniques as **alliteration** and **onomatopoeia**, which poets also use for effect. Here is a basic list that you may (or may not) remember:

alliteration: when a number of words in quick succession begin with the same letter or the same letter is repeated. For example, *Full fathom five thy father lies*, as Ariel sings in *The Tempest*.

assonance: similar to alliteration, but now with the repetition of vowel sounds. For example, *And so, all the night-tide, I lie down by the side/ Of my darling—my darling—my life and my bride,/ In the sepulchre there by the sea,/ In her tomb by the sounding sea.* (Edgar Allan Poe, *Annabel Lee*)

euphemism: replacing an unpleasant word or concept with something less offensive, as in substituting the term *Grim Reaper* for *death*. Some are also intended to be funny, as when morticians refer to *corpses* as *clients*.

hyperbole: Pronounced hy-PER-bo-lee. Not HY-per-bowl. Exaggeration for effect, as in *I've told you a hundred times*. This is the opposite of...

litotes: understatement for effect, as when *not bad* means *completely wonderful*. Litotes can be interpreted differently, depending on culture and verbal emphasis.

metaphor: an expression in which a word is used in a nonliteral sense, saying that *x is y* rather than *x is like y*, which would be a simile. For example, Macbeth's *Life's but a walking shadow, a poor player, That struts and frets his hour upon the stage.*

metonymy: *Merriam-Webster* defines this as "a figure of speech consisting of the name of one thing for that of another of which it is an attribute or with which it is associated." For example, the term *press*, which originally was used for printing press, now connotates the news media. Easily confused with synecdoche.

onomatopoeia: a word or phrase that sounds (a bit) like the sound it is meant to convey: *buzz, purr,* or Tennyson's *the murmuring of innumerable bees.*

oxymoron: an apparent contradiction for effect, the classic example being *jumbo shrimp.*

personification: giving human qualities, such as emotions, desires, and sensations to an inanimate object or an abstract idea. Emily Dickinson's *The Railway Train* is often cited as an example of personification:

> *I like to see it lap the miles,*
> *And lick the valleys up,*
> *And stop to feed itself at tanks;*
> *And then, prodigious step*
> *Around a pile of mountains...*

simile: a comparison that—unlike a metaphor—expresses itself as a comparison, usually with the words *as* or *like.* Examples include *dead as a dodo* or *like a bat out of hell.*

synecdoche: a form of metonymy, but in this instance specifically "a whole for the part or a part for the whole." For example, *a set of wheels* used to denote the term *automobile,* or the command *All hands on deck* to summon a crew of sailors.

Prosody

Confusingly, prosody has nothing to do with prose—it is defined by *Merriam-Webster* as "the study of versification; especially: the systematic study of metrical structure."

The basic unit of a line of poetry—normally comprising two or three syllables—is called a **foot**, and the most common feet are:

iamb (adj. **iambic**): a short syllable followed by a long one. The most widely used foot in English poetry. Much of Shakespeare's verse is written in *iambic pentameter,* which means that a line consists of five iambic feet, or ten syllables in all:

Shall I / compare/ thee to/ a sum/ mer's day?
(*Sonnet 43*)

If mu/ sic be/ the food/ of love,/ play on
(*Twelfth Night*)

trochee: a long syllable followed by a short one, although the final syllable is often missing:

*Tiger!/ Tiger!/ burning/ bright
In the/ forest / of the/ night*
(Blake, *The Tiger*)

dactyl: a long syllable followed by two short ones (again, the final syllable is often dropped). It produces a gentle, flowing rhythm:

*This is the/ forest prim/ eval. The/ murmuring/
pines and the/ hemlocks*

(Longfellow, *Evangeline*)

anapest: two short syllables followed by a long one. In contrast to a dactyl, this conveys pace and action. It is often used in comic verses such as the nonsense poem by Lewis Caroll, *The Hunting of the Snark:*

> *In the midst of the word he was trying to say/ In the midst of his laughter and glee/ He had softly and suddenly vanished away/ For the Snark <u>was</u> Boojum, you see.*

spondee: two long syllables, giving a heavy, rhythmical effect. The following example combines spondee and trochee so that you can almost hear the soldiers marching along:

> *We're / foot—slog/ —slog—slog/ —sloggin'/ over/ Africa—*
>
> *Foot—foot/—foot—foot/—sloggin'/ over/ Africa—*
>
> *(Boots—boots/—boots—boots/—movin'/ up and/ down a/ gain!)*

(Kipling, *Boots*)

LITERATURE

Oh, those dreadful textbooks and anthologies. Who could ever forget the detailed chapter on tying knots in *Moby Dick?* Perhaps *Julius Caesar* was your particular nemesis. On the other hand, *Macbeth, Frankenstein,* and just about any of Poe's dark stories could deliciously disturb your evenings for nights on end. After all, as a teenager, it was sometimes hard to immerse yourself in the literature of serious life-and-death situations. So here's your second chance.

British Authors and Playwrights

There are some authors who embody the definition of "classic" literature. We all recognize the names: Austen, the Brontë sisters, Dickens, and Shakespeare. However, could you pass a pop quiz on their greatest works? Here's a brief rundown to review—just in case.

☞ JANE AUSTEN (1775–1817)

Jane Austen completed only six novels, which makes it easy to do a rundown of her complete works. In no particular order:

Emma: Emma Woodhouse is the most important young lady in her village, living alone with her aging father (the one who thinks that the sooner any party breaks up the better). Clever and pleased with herself, she amuses herself with matchmaking.

Despite the disapproval of her friend and neighbor, Mr. Knightley, she persuades her protégée, Harriet Smith, not to marry a respectable farmer, Robert Martin, thinking that Harriet (despite being poor, ignorant, and illegitimate) should set her sights on the new vicar, Mr. Elton. Mr. Elton, however, has set his sights on Emma and is deeply offended when she rejects him. He promptly marries someone else entirely, and Harriet, recovering from her disappointment, falls in love with Mr. Knightley instead. Emma's eyes are suddenly opened to the fact that no one should marry Mr. Knightley but herself. Fortunately, this turns out to be what he has always wanted.

Mansfield Park: Jane Austen's least appealing heroine is the virtuous but dull Fanny Price, who is sent to live at Mansfield Park with her aunt, Lady Bertram, and promptly falls in love with her cousin Edmund, another deeply virtuous person. The arrival of the worldly Crawfords, brother and sister Henry and Mary, upsets the calm of the neighborhood, with Edmund becoming smitten with Mary despite his disapproval of her character, and Henry attracting the attention of both Bertram sisters, Maria and Julia, despite the fact that both have admirers of their own. Henry, however, falls in love with Fanny, who is almost persuaded that her good influence can redeem his character, but then he elopes with Maria, now Mrs. Rushworth. Amid all the scandal and disappointment, Edmund finally recognizes Fanny's worth.

Northanger Abbey: Catherine Morland's head is full of ghoulish Gothic novels, so when she is invited to Northanger Abbey by her friend Elinor Tilney (with whose brother, Henry, she is already in love), she thinks she has discovered a horrific mystery: Elinor's father, the general, has murdered his wife. It turns out to be nonsense, of course, and she is deeply embarrassed that Henry should know of her silly suspicions. General Tilney now discovers that Catherine is not, as he has been led to believe, an heiress, and turns her out of the house. She is back at home thinking gloomy thoughts about her future when Henry appears and...

Persuasion: Eight years before the novel starts, Anne Elliot was persuaded by her proud father, Sir Walter, and her well-meaning friend Lady Russell to break off her engagement to Captain Frederick Wentworth. Now twenty-six, she has never met anyone else she can care for (and indeed has turned down a proposal from a neighbor, Charles Musgrove, who subsequently marries her sister, Mary). Chance brings Captain Wentworth, now wealthy, back into the neighborhood, but throws him together with Charles Musgrove's sisters, Henrietta and Louisa. Anne is forced to watch in silence as he apparently becomes involved with Louisa, whose steadfastness of character seems to appeal to him more than the weakness he has not forgiven in Anne. An outing to Lyme Regis ends with Louisa insisting on jumping off the Cobb, falling and causing herself serious injury. Just as Captain Wentworth's feelings toward Anne are reawakening, he finds that all his friends believe he is committed to Louisa, and he cannot honorably renege on this perceived promise. But Louisa, in the course of her convalescence, conveniently falls in love with Captain Wentworth's friend Captain Benwick, and Wentworth is free again.

Pride and Prejudice: Spirited but poor Elizabeth Bennet (Lizzy) takes a stand against the proud but extremely wealthy Mr. Darcy, particularly when he destroys the chances of her sister Jane marrying his friend Mr. Bingley. Darcy falls in love with Lizzy much against his better judgment and is tactless enough to tell her so. Scandal hits the Bennet family when the youngest daughter, Lydia, elopes with the charming but feckless Wickham, but Darcy saves the day. An unlikely scenario for bringing lovers together, but it does, as many readers predict, and the two "deserving" daughters make the happy marriages at the end of the novel. After all, "a single man in possession of good fortune must be in want of a wife."

Other characters include two more Bennet sisters, plain and studious Mary and silly Kitty; their parents, the empty-headed Mrs. Bennet and introverted, sarcastic Mr. Bennet; Mr. Bennet's cousin and heir, the bumbling clergyman Mr. Collins; and his haughty patroness Lady Catherine de Bourgh, who also happens to be Darcy's aunt.

Sense and Sensibility: The Dashwood sisters, Elinor and Marianne, are completely different in temperament, and, when Marianne falls in love with the dashing Willoughby, the whole world knows it. Elinor, on the other hand, suffers her disappointment over Edward Ferrars in silence. Willoughby is summoned to London just as he appears to be on the brink of proposing to Marianne and instead becomes engaged to a wealthy woman. Marianne's heartbreak is eventually healed by the less dashing Colonel Brandon, and Elinor gets Edward in the end.

Jane Austen also wrote fragments of two other novels, *The Watsons* and *Sanditon,* which have been published in their incomplete forms and variously completed by other authors.

☞ THE BRONTËS
There were three sisters who wrote novels—Anne (1820–49), Charlotte (1816–55), and Emily (1818–48). All, especially

Emily, were also poets of some distinction. Charlotte wrote *Shirley, Villette,* and *The Professor,* but her most famous novel is *Jane Eyre:*

***Jane Eyre* by Charlotte Brontë:** A poor orphan girl secures a job as governess to the ward of Mr. Rochester at Thornfield Manor, a place where strange noises tend to emanate from the attic. Jane and Rochester fall in love, but their wedding is stopped by the intervention of Mr. Mason, who announces that Rochester is, in fact, married to his sister, Bertha. And indeed he is, but she is mad and confined to the attic and watched over by the fearsome Grace Poole. Jane runs away and seeks refuge with her cousins, the Rivers; on the point of accepting a proposal of marriage from St. John Rivers, she thinks she hears Rochester calling her and insists on returning to Thornfield. There she finds that Bertha has broken out of her attic, set fire to the house, perished in the flames, and left Rochester blind, disfigured, and dependent. "Reader," as she famously says, "I married him."

***The Tenant of Wildfell Hall* by Anne Brontë:** Although Anne wrote *Agnes Gray,* a story about the horrors of being a governess in Victorian England, *The Tenant of Wildfell Hall* is slightly better known, perhaps for its public-television BBC series. This work could exemplify one of the first feminist novels, since it illustrates the inequities sometimes evident between men and women in marriage. The story involves the arrival of a mysterious new tenant, Helen Huntingdon, who with her young son moves to a small village in Yorkshire. A farmer falls in love with her, only to learn that she is still married to a wealthy man back in London. The husband becomes ill, inevitably from his life of debauchery, and eventually dies, leaving Helen free. You can likely guess what happens next.

Wuthering Heights **by Emily Brontë:** This *extremely* dark tale of unrequited, misguided love and revenge oftentimes reaks with an uncomfortable intensity. Heathcliff is a wild orphan brought home to Wuthering Heights by kindly Mr. Earnshaw, Cathy's father. The two fall passionately in love, but Cathy refuses to marry a nobody and instead marries their drippy neighbor, Edgar Linton. Heathcliff, in revenge, marries Edgar's sister, Isabella, and cruelly mistreats her. Cathy dies in childbirth. Heathcliff goes a bit bonkers and ends up pretty much killing himself so as to be reunited with Cathy in death.

☞ **CHARLES DICKENS (1812–70)**
Love him or hate him, Dickens inspired many great films, and everyone knows what *Dickensian* means.

A Christmas Carol: The miserly Ebenezer Scrooge tries to ignore Christmas and is haunted by the ghost of his former partner, Marley, and by the ghosts of Christmases Past, Present, and Yet to Come, who show him the error of his ways.

David Copperfield: Dickens's favorite—the life story of a boy who is sent to boarding school by his evil stepfather, runs away to his eccentric aunt, becomes a lawyer, and then a writer. Sounds pretty dull, but really it is about growing up, learning from experience, and coming to terms with life. It's full of colorful characters such as Mr. Micawber, always hoping that something will turn up; the ever so 'umble Uriah Heep; Aunt Betsy Trotwood; and her mad companion, Mr. Dick, who is obsessed with the execution of Charles I; not to mention the Peggotty family, the deeply drippy Dora, and the saintly Agnes.

Oliver Twist: About the boy from the workhouse who is kicked out after he "wants some more" food and finds his way into a gang of pickpockets led by Fagin. The novel contains considerably more misery and rather less singing and dancing than the musical version.

If you don't remember much about Dickens, chances are most of the characters you do recall are from the ones previously mentioned from *David Copperfield;* the Artful Dodger, Nancy, the evil Bill Sikes, and Mr. Bumble the beadle from *Oliver Twist;* and Bob Cratchit and Tiny Tim from *A Christmas Carol.* But here are a few more stories that may ring bells:

The plot of *Bleak House* centers around the ongoing case of Jarndyce vs. Jarndyce, which eventually eats up all the money that is being disputed; the Circumlocution Office, Dickens's savage attack on civil service bureaucracy, appears in *Little Dorrit;* and *Barnaby Rudge* is set against the background of the Gordon Riots (anti-Catholic riots in London in 1780).

~~~~~~

☞ SHAKESPEARE (1564–1616)

William Shakespeare wrote 37 plays, 154 sonnets, and a number of much longer poems. There isn't room in this book to summarize all the plays, so here are—arguably—the 10 best known.

Hamlet, Prince of Denmark: Another one where everyone dies. Hamlet's father, also Hamlet, has died in suspicious circumstances, and his widow, Gertrude, has married—with indecent haste—Hamlet senior's brother, Claudius. The ghost of King Hamlet tells his son that he has been murdered by

Claudius. Prince Hamlet then spends much of the play worrying about what to do and talking to himself—hence all the famous soliloquies. He has previously been attached to Ophelia, daughter of Polonius, the lord chamberlain, but he now rejects her ("Get thee to a nunnery"). Talking to his mother in her room, Hamlet realizes that someone is eavesdropping behind a wall hanging, and Hamlet stabs the individual, believing it to be Claudius. It is, in fact, Polonius. Ophelia goes mad and drowns herself. Her brother, Laertes, is determined to avenge his family, so Claudius arranges a fencing match in which Laertes will have a poisoned sword. Laertes wounds Hamlet; then there is a scuffle in which the two exchange swords and Hamlet wounds Laertes. Knowing that he is dying, Laertes confesses, Hamlet stabs Claudius, and Gertrude drinks poisoned wine that Claudius had prepared as a fallback for outing Hamlet. "Good night, sweet prince," says his friend Horatio as he prepares to clear up the mess.

Hamlet contains more quotations than the other plays. For example, Polonius's paternal advice to his son Laertes:

> Neither a borrower nor a lender be:
> For loan oft loses both itself and friend;
> And borrowing dulls the edge of husbandry.
> This above all—to thine own self be true;
> And it must follow, as the night the day,
> Thou canst not then be false to any man.

And a bit of Hamlet's most famous soliloquy…

> To be, or not to be; that is the question:
> Whether 'tis nobler in the mind to suffer
> The slings and arrows of outrageous fortune,

Or to take arms against a sea of troubles,
And by opposing end them? To die, to sleep;
No more; and by a sleep to say we end
The heart-ache and the thousand natural shocks
That flesh is heir to,—'tis a consummation
Devoutly to be wish'd. To die, to sleep;
To sleep! Perchance to dream: ay, there's the rub;
For in that sleep of death what dreams may come,
When we have shuffled off this mortal coil,
Must give us pause.

Julius Caesar: A number of Roman citizens, notably Caesar's close friend Marcus Brutus and his brother, Cassius, are worried that Caesar is becoming too powerful, so they kill him ("*Et tu, Brute?* Then fall Caesar"). But that happens in Act III Scene I, only halfway through the play. The rest is about the fallout from the assassination: the vengeance wrought on the conspirators by Caesar's supporters, led by Mark Antony; the conflict between Brutus and Cassius (the one who has "a lean and hungry look—he thinks too much; such men are dangerous."); the effect on them and their feelings of guilt; and their eventual defeat and suicide. And speaking of rabble-rousing, Antony's funeral oration, which works the crowd up into a frenzy so that they will avenge the murder, runs fairly close to *Henry V:*

Friends, Romans, countrymen; lend me your ears;
I come to bury Caesar, not to praise him...
He was my friend, faithful and just to me:
But Brutus says he was ambitious;
And Brutus is an honorable man...

and so on and so forth, until the mob is fairly baying for Brutus's blood.

King Lear: Lear is "the foolish, fond old man" who decides to retire and divide his kingdom among his three daughters, Goneril, Regan, and Cordelia. The two eldest make fancy speeches about loving their father above all else; Cordelia refuses to play this game and is promptly exiled. Lear plans to spend half his time with Goneril and half with Regan, but these two wicked sisters have other ideas and soon kick him out. He wanders around in the rain, goes mad, meets up with Cordelia again, and then everyone dies. There is a subplot concerning the Earl of Gloucester's bastard son Edmund, who plots against everyone and becomes betrothed to both Goneril and Regan (despite the fact that they are both married). They all die, too.

Macbeth: The Scottish play. Three witches prophesy that Macbeth will become Thane of Cawdor and subsequently king. When he is proclaimed Thane of Cawdor, he starts wondering about hurrying the second prophecy along. Egged on by his wife, he murders King Duncan and is proclaimed king in his place. And it's all downhill from there. One murder leads to another, he is haunted by guilt (personified by the ghost of his friend Banquo, who appears at a banquet), Lady Macbeth goes mad and dies (after the famous "Out damned spot" hand-washing/sleepwalking scene), and Macbeth is finally killed in battle. Ultimately, Duncan's son Malcolm is restored to the throne.

The Merchant of Venice: Shylock the Jewish moneylender hates Antonio the Christian merchant. When Antonio needs to borrow money from him to help out his friend Bassanio, Shylock makes him sign a bond promising that he will pay

Shylock one pound of his own flesh should he fail to repay the loan. Bassanio takes the money and successfully courts the wealthy Portia. Antonio's ships are lost at sea, and he is unable to pay Shylock, who claims his pound of flesh. Portia disguises herself as a lawyer and rescues Antonio by pointing out that, contractually, Shylock is entitled to take a pound of flesh but no blood—a logistical impossibility. Her speech beginning "The quality of mercy is not strained" comes from this scene. A happy ending—unless you are Shylock.

A Midsummer Night's Dream: The one about the fairies. Three plots interwoven: In a wood outside Athens, two pairs of young lovers brush up against the squabbling king and queen of the fairies, Oberon and Titania, and Oberon's servant Puck. In the same wood a group of workmen, including Bottom the Weaver, are rehearsing the play *Pyramus and Thisbe* to perform at the forthcoming wedding of the Duke of Athens. Oberon has a magic potion that, when squeezed on the eyelids of someone who is asleep, makes that person fall in love with the first object he or she sees upon awakening. As a result, Titania falls in love with Bottom, whom Puck has given an ass's head, and Puck confuses the young lovers so that they keep falling in and out of love with the wrong partners. But in the end "all is mended."

Othello, the Moor of Venice: Othello is a successful general, but the problem is that he is black and has secretly married a white girl, Desdemona. The other problem is that Iago hates him, partly because Othello has promoted a young lieutenant, Cassio, over Iago's head. Iago persuades Othello that Cassio is having an affair with Desdemona. Mad with jealousy ("the green-eyed monster"), Othello smothers Desdemona in her bed. Iago also tries to have Cassio murdered, but the plot fails, and letters proving Iago's guilt and Cassio's innocence are discovered. Othello realizes that he has murdered Desdemona for no reason and kills himself. Othello was the man who loved "not wisely but too well," and it was Iago who said, "Who steals my purse steals trash." (But he was lying, of course.)

This section ends with words from one famous sonnet—number 18—whose first four lines have provided titles for at least two novels:

> Shall I compare thee to a summer's day?
> Thou art more lovely and more temperate;
> Rough winds do shake the darling buds of May,
> And summer's lease hath all too short a date.

Romeo and Juliet: The original star-crossed lovers. Romeo is a Montague, Juliet a Capulet, and the two families hate each other. Romeo and Juliet secretly marry. However, Juliet has already been commissioned to marry her cousin, Paris. To get out of this, Juliet comes up with one of those clever schemes that you just know will go wrong: She takes a potion that puts her into a coma for a couple of days so that everyone thinks she is dead. The message telling Romeo about this goes astray (of course), and he arrives at her tomb believing that she is dead. He poisons himself just before she wakes up, so Juliet, discovering him dead, stabs herself with his dagger.

The balcony scene is full of famous lines. For example, when Romeo lurks in the garden, Juliet appears on the balcony above and, talking to herself, says:

O Romeo, Romeo! Wherefore art thou Romeo?...
What's in a name? That which we call a rose,
By any other name would smell as sweet.

And at the end of the scene, she says:

Good-night, good-night! Parting is such sweet sorrow
That I shall say good-night till it be morrow.

The Taming of the Shrew: Katharina is too bad-tempered to secure a husband, but her father will not allow her younger (and better behaved) sister, Bianca, to accept any of her many suitors until Katharina is married. Petruchio comes along and accepts the challenge, more or less beating Kate into submission. Twenty-first-century feminists do not care for this play, although Cole Porter's musical version, *Kiss Me Kate,* is wonderful.

Twelfth Night: Twins Viola and Sebastian become separated in a storm, and each believes the other dead. Viola disguises herself as a boy, Cesario, and enters the service of Duke Orsino, with whom she falls in love. Orsino, however, is in love with Olivia and uses Cesario as a messenger to woo her. Olivia—you guessed it—falls in love with Cesario, and it takes the reappearance of Sebastian to make everyone live happily ever after. The subplot concerns Olivia's pompous steward, Malvolio, who is conned by Olivia's uncle and his friends into believing that Olivia is in love with him and that she wishes to see him wearing yellow stockings and cross garters. The well-known saying "Some are born great, some achieve greatness, and some have greatness thrust upon them" appears in the letter that Malvolio believes Olivia has written to him.

Other Notable British Authors

Name	Major Works	Notes
William Blake (1757–1827) poet and artist	*Songs of Innocence*	Painter, and a bit of a religious upstart.
The Brownings, Elizabeth Barrett (1806–1861) and **Robert** (1812–1889) poets	"How Do I Love Thee" from *Sonnets for the Portuguese*, and "Grow Old Along with Me" from *Rabbi Ben Ezra*	Secretly married in 1846. He loved her despite her frail health. In 1861 she died in her husband's arms.
Sir Arthur Conan Doyle (1859–1930)	Sherlock Holmes stories, *The Lost World*	Started writing when his medical practice slowed.
George Eliot (1819–1880) pen name	*Middlemarch, Silas Marner*	Real name was Mary Ann Evans, but she changed it so her work would be taken more seriously; also because of her relationship with a married man.
E. M. Forster (1879–1970)	*A Room with a View, Howards End, Where Angels Fear to Tread, A Passage to India, The Longest Journey, Maurice*	Recent PBS series, *A Room with a View*, contained an alternative ending. Most of his novels were adapted for film.
John Galsworthy (1867–1933)	*The Forsyte Saga* and its sequels	Pulitzer Prize for Literature, 1932. People skipped church to see the BBC adaptation of *The Forsyte Saga* in the 1960s!
William Golding (1911–1993)	*Lord of the Flies, Pincher Martin, Darkness Visible, To the Ends of the Earth*	Was in D-Day invasion in Normandy. Won Booker Prize and Nobel Prize. Knighted by Queen Elizabeth II.
Ted Hughes (1930–1998) poet	*Crow, Tales from Ovid, Birthday Letters*	Poet Laureate. Married to Sylvia Plath. Great poet but merciless philanderer.

Name	Major Works	Notes
D. H. Lawrence (1885–1930)	*Sons and Lovers, The Rainbow, Women in Love, Lady Chatterley's Lover*	His work, considered scandalous for its time, was burned and banned.
C. S. Lewis (1898–1963) Irish-born	*The Chronicles of Narnia, A Grief Observed, Mere Christianity, The Allegory of Love*	*The Lion, the Witch, and the Wardrobe* and *Prince Caspian* recently adapted for film.
Christopher Marlowe (1564–1593) playwright, poet	*Edward II, Doctor Faustus, The Passionate Shepherd to His Love* ("Come live with me and be my love and we will all the pleasures prove")	Killed in Deptford tavern; some speculate that he spied for Elizabeth I. Freethinker and contemporary to Shakespeare.
Somerset Maugham (1874–1965)	*Of Human Bondage, The Razor's Edge, The Moon and Sixpence*	WWI spy; *Ashenden* influenced Ian Fleming's Bond series.
George Orwell, (1903–1950) pen name	*Animal Farm, 1984*	Real name was Eric Arthur Blair; died of tuberculosis at 46.
Alexander Pope (1688-1744) poet	"A Little Learning is a dangerous thing." *Essay on Man, The Rape of the Lock*	Also from *Essay on Man;* "To err is human, to forgive, divine."
Robert Louis Stevenson (1850–1894) Scottish	*Treasure Island, A Child's Garden of Verses*	Loved to travel despite poor health. Died at 44.
Jonathan Swift (1667–1745) Anglo-Irish	*Gulliver's Travels*	Wrote his own obituary.
J. R. R. Tolkien (1892–1973)	*The Hobbit, The Lord of the Rings*	"All that is gold does not glitter; not all those that wander are lost."
Virginia Woolf (1882–1941)	*A Room of One's Own, Mrs. Dalloway, To the Lighthouse, Orlando*	Filled her pockets with stones and drowned herself in the River Ouse.

North American Authors

There is a countless number of American writers who have earned their rightful place in literary history. While it is tricky to capture all of them in one relatively brief chapter, here are some that many students have come to know very well.

~~~~~~

☞ **PEARL BUCK** (1892–1973)

Winner of both the Nobel Prize in Literature and the Pulitzer Prize, Buck wrote more than 100 titles, as well as short stories, plays, a book of verse, children's books, biographies, and a cookbook—much while sitting in her office at her Bucks County, Pennsylvania farmhouse watching her eight children play outside her window. Brought to China from Virginia as a young girl, Buck lived among the missionaries and based much of her work on her travels to Asia. In addition to the best-selling The *Good Earth,* a few other works by Buck include *Dragon Seed, East Wind: West Wind,* and the *House of Earth* trilogy. She also founded the charitable organization Pearl S. Buck International, which helps children around the world who have been marginalized due to mixed heredity, disease, hunger, poverty, or other tragic circumstances.

~~~~~~

☞ **STEPHEN CRANE** (1871–1900)

Writer and journalist, Crane died at 28 years old and will forever be remembered for the required-reading novel, the *Red Badge of Courage,* which details the horrors of war experienced by a young soldier. This classic is based on memoirs and interviews with Civil War veterans.

☞ RALPH WALDO EMERSON (1803–82)

Essayist, philosopher, abolitionist, and poet, Emerson greatly influenced the transcendentalist movement of the mid-1800s. His associations include Henry David Thoreau (Walden Pond was on his property) and Nathaniel Hawthorne and his neighbor Louisa May Alcott. His collected essays included "Self-Reliance," which warned people to avoid conformity and to follow their own ideas and instincts. "Nature," "Circles," and "The Poet" are a few of his other most successful pieces.

☞ WILLIAM FAULKNER (1897–1962)

Known for his stream of consciousness, Faulkner's literary technique depicts what is going on in the speaker's head rather than simply relating the person's dialogue with others. In his novel *As I Lay Dying*, Faulkner presents 15 different points of view. Other well-known novels include *The Sound and the Fury; Light in August; Absalom, Absalom;* and *The Unvanquished.*

☞ F. SCOTT FITZGERALD (1896–1940)

Francis Scott Key Fitzgerald was the namesake and second cousin three times removed of the author of the United States' National Anthem. His six finished novels, including *Tender Is the Night* and *This Side of Paradise* and many short stories evoke the Jazz Age and his tumultuous relationship with his wife, Zelda Sayre. Like a fine wine, his masterpiece *The Great Gatsby* is about the futility and moral decay of the wealthy that gets even better with age. Fitzgerald died at 44, considering himself a failed writer. However, *Gatsby* continues as a best seller and is often required reading for many high school and college students.

☞ NATHANIEL HAWTHORNE (1804–1864)

Who could forget the *Scarlet Letter*'s all-too-human Hester Prynne, who—after being separated from her cool-hearted husband (Chillingworth)—has a passionate affair with her charismatic minister. The Puritans chide her and force her to wear a scarlet "A" upon her breast, advertising her sin. Hester dutifully (and wisely) protects Pastor Dimmesdale from public scorn, but his conscience catches up to him. The story warns of the scourge of sin and that people can be downright self-righteous. A few other examples from his published works include *The House of the Seven Gables;* a short-story collection, *Twice-Told Tales,* and the short stories "The Birthmark" and "Young Goodman Brown."

☞ JOSEPH HELLER (1923–1999)

Although he is often regarded as one of the best post-World War II satirists, Heller's career included stints as a blacksmith's apprentice, a B-25 bombardier, and an advertising copywriter. However, his novel *Catch-22* is one of the few whose title has created an idiom rather than employing an existing quotation. The plot centers on a group of American fighter pilots in Italy during World War II and their efforts to avoid flying suicidal missions. The problem is that the only way they can get out of flying missions is if they are crazy—but the moment they ask to be grounded because flying the missions is crazy, they are deemed to be entirely sane, and therefore fit to fly.

☞ ERNEST HEMINGWAY (1899–1961)

Remember the determined Santiago, the aging Cuban fisherman who struggles with a marlin in the Gulf Stream? *The Old Man and the Sea* won the Nobel Prize in Literature in 1954 and has been heavily analyzed in classrooms for its symbolism ever since. Hemingway, however, is posthumously quoted in a 1999 issue of *Time* ("An American Storyteller") as saying, "No good book has ever been written that has in it symbols arrived at beforehand and stuck in…. I tried to make a real old man, a real boy, a real sea and a real fish and real sharks. But if I made them good and true enough, they would mean many things." Hemingway was frank and wickedly tough, evident in some of his other great works: *The Sun Also Rises, A Farewell to Arms,* and *For Whom the Bell Tolls.*

☞ ZORA NEALE HURSTON (1891–1960)

Once criticized for her cultural depictions and political views, Hurston's work, *Their Eyes Were Watching God,* has grown into a seminal work for African-American and feminist writers, and it is a darn good read. The story relates the struggles of Janie Sparks, who in the end says, "Two things everybody got tuh do fuh theyselves. They got tuh go tuh God, and they got tuh find out about livin' fuh theyselves." Hurston's work grew from the Harlem Renaissance and was revived in the 1970s after an article in *Ms.* by *Color Purple* author Alice Walker.

☞ WASHINGTON IRVING (1783–1859)

Known for the *Legend of Sleepy Hollow,* which tells of the unfortunate disappearance of Ichabod Crane one autumn night after being pursued by the infamous headless horseman (the ghost of a Hessian soldier who had his head blown off during the American Revolution). Irving also wrote the Grimm-influenced (some say stolen) *Rip Van Winkle,* where a henpecked husband who hates his honey-do list heads for the hills. He then takes the drink of some bowling ghosts and falls asleep for a mere 20 years, waking up to a changed geographical and political landscape, a foot-long beard, and a deceased wife. Rip, however, resumes his old walks and habits.

☞ **HENRY JAMES** (1843–1916)
Although born in New York City, James eventually settled in England, becoming a British subject shortly before his death. James often wrote books that crossed the continents. *The Portrait of a Lady* was adapted for film in 1996, directed by Jane Campion. The story involves a newly wealthy, young American woman who travels to Europe and becomes scammed into marriage by two U.S. expatriates. James's other admired works include *Washington Square, The Bostonians,* and his shorter pieces, "The Aspern Papers," and "The Turn of the Screw."

☞ **HARPER LEE** (1926–)
Born in Monroeville, Alabama, Lee was a childhood friend and next-door neighbor of novelist Truman Capote. In 1956 some close friends gave her a year's salary for Christmas so she could take the time to write. Within that time she wrote one book, *To Kill a Mockingbird,* which was published in 1960 and won the Pulitzer Prize for fiction in 1961. The novel depicts the story of a white lawyer in a Deep South town who defends a black man who is wrongly accused of raping a white girl.

☞ HERMAN MELVILLE (1819–91)

You either love him or hate him, but one thing is for sure: After you read *Moby Dick,* you will know how to tie several different knots. Melville's immense detail and multileveled symbolism combine to make what is often called the epitome of American Romanticism (of epic proportions). The first chapter opens with the famous line "Call me Ishmael." Then soon the reader is afloat on this vessel as it ventures forth, fighting to surmount both fate and nature. Melville wrote other works, such as *Pierre* and the unfinished *Billy Budd.*

☞ LUCY MAUD MONTGOMERY (1874–1942)

Her works would become a favorite of young women around the world, and whose famous protagonist Anne Shirley once said, "Marilla, isn't it nice to think that tomorrow is a new day with no mistakes in it yet?" Some other "Anne" books include: *Anne of Green Gables, Anne of Avonlea, Anne of the Island, Anne of Windy Poplars,* and *Anne's House of Dreams.* In 1985 a miniseries based on her first novel was among one of the highest-rated programs of any genre to air on Canadian television and won several awards. The films starred Megan Follows as Anne and Colleen Dewhurst as Marilla Cuthbert.

☞ EDGAR ALLAN POE (1809–1849)

Poe's major success, *The Raven,* was published two years before the death of his first wife (his 13-year-old first cousin). After this unfortunate event and scandalous allegations of amorous indiscretions, Poe became dejected and began drinking. Two years later he was scraped off the streets of Baltimore, sick and delirious, and he died soon after. His wife's death influenced his writing, such as in *Annabel Lee*. Poe has a long list of bone-chilling stories, including *The Cask of Amontillado, The Fall of the House of Usher, The Masque of the Red Death,* and *The Pit and the Pendulum*. Many of his tales were adapted for film in the 1960s and starred horror legend Vincent Price.

☞ J. D. SALINGER (1919–)

The reclusive Salinger's biggest success is *The Catcher in the Rye,* the ultimate disaffected-teenager novel. It is told in the first person by sixteen-year-old Holden Caulfield, who loathes everything to do with his life and his parents' "phony" middle-class values. Although the novel was written in 1951, it remains popular and sells approximately 250,000 copies a year.

☞ JOHN STEINBECK (1920–68)

While growing up Steinbeck worked as a hired hand on nearby ranches, which fostered his impressions of the California countryside and its people. These thoughts contributed to the Pulitzer Prize-winning novel, *The Grapes of Wrath*. The book tells the story of the Joad family, who after the Oklahoma dust bowl disaster of the 1930s abandon their land and head for what they imagine is "Promised Land" in California, only to find that life is no easier there. His novels *Tortilla Flat* and *Cannery Row* also achieved critical acclaim.

☞ HARRIET BEECHER STOWE (1811–96)

Best known as the author of *Uncle Tom's Cabin,* a violent antislavery novel (published in 1852, when this was *the* political hot potato in America). According to legend, when Abraham Lincoln met Stowe in 1862 he said, "So you're the little woman who wrote the book that started this Great War!" Her writing career spanned 51 years, during which she published 30 books and countless shorter pieces as well as raising seven children. A year after she and her family moved into their Hartford, Connecticut house, Samuel Clemens, also known as Mark Twain, moved into a house just across the lawn.

☞ HENRY DAVID THOREAU (1817–62)

Sometimes called the father of environmentalism, he stated, "Thank God men cannot fly and lay waste the sky as well as the earth." He retreated to the woodland, isolating himself from society and wrote *Walden,* an account of simple living in natural surroundings. He also wrote an essay on Civil Disobedience after being arrested for not paying his taxes, which he did to protest slavery and the Mexican-American War.

☞ MARK TWAIN (1835–1910)
(Samuel Langhorne Clemens)

Drawing on his experience as a river pilot, this author's pen name comes from a riverboat term for two fathoms or 12 feet when the depth of water is sounded; "Mark twain" means that it is safe to navigate. Although Twain was also a popular humorist, satirist, and lecturer, he is best known as the author of *The Adventures of Tom Sawyer,* which drew on his childhood in the Mississippi River port of Hannibal, Missouri, and *The Adventures of Huckleberry Finn,* a much more serious book—sometimes called the Great American Novel—that had the issue of slavery at its heart.

☞ BOOKER T. WASHINGTON (1856–1915)

A former slave, freed after the Civil War, this author and educator worked tirelessly through school. He later became a noted educator and major proponent of education and rights for African Americans, working to establish vocational schools so they could learn trades, obtain jobs, and bolster their standing in society. The details of his life can be found in his compelling autobiography and best seller, *Up from Slavery.*

☞ EDITH WHARTON (1862–1937)

She became the first woman to win the Pulitzer Prize for Literature in 1921, for *The Age of Innocence,* which deals with upper-class society in New York City during the turn of the century, where marriage for connection was encouraged. Wharton could subtly poke fun at the upper classes, while displaying a warm, sympathetic tone. She had ample time and opportunity to observe her subjects, since her maiden name was Edith Newbold Jones, the wealthy family associated with the adage "Keeping up with the Joneses." Some of her other notable works include *The House of Mirth, Ethan Frome,* and her unfinished work (finished in 1993 by Marion Mainwaring) *The Buccaneers,* which was adapted for Masterpiece Theatre in 1995—a series that was soon forgotten.

British Poets

The myths, legends, and romance of the major British poets have sparked millions of imaginations. The following list mentions just a handful of the most familiar ones.

☞ **W(YSTAN) H(UGH) AUDEN** (1907–73, English)
Shot to renewed fame 20 years after his death, thanks to the film *Four Weddings and a Funeral*. *Stop all the clocks, cut off the telephone,* which is recited at the funeral, is taken from his "Twelve Songs."

☞ **ROBERT BURNS** (1759–96, determinedly Scottish)
His birthday was January 25, and for some reason many people still celebrate the event by eating haggis and reciting his poetry. In addition to the wonderfully bloodthirsty "Address to a Haggis," he also wrote "To a Mouse" (*Wee sleekit, cow'rin' tim'rous beastie* and *The best laid schemes o' mice an' men/ Gang aft a-gley*) and the words of *Auld Lang Syne*.

☞ **GEORGE GORDON BYRON, LORD BYRON**
   (1788–1824, English/Scottish)
The one who *awoke one morning and found myself famous* after the publication of *Childe Harold's Pilgrimage*. He led a wild life, left England after one scandal too many, lived in Italy, where he was friendly with Shelley, then fought for Greek insurgents against the Turks. He died at Missolonghi, in Greece, of rheumatic fever.

☞ GEOFFREY CHAUCER (c.1340–1400, English)

Chaucer is credited as being one of the first great poets to write in English rather than in French or Latin. Although his language is pretty unfamiliar to the uninitiated, he is best known for *The Canterbury Tales,* in which a party of outrageous pilgrims travel from the Tabard Inn in Southwark, London, to Canterbury Cathedral, where they tell stories to pass the time. The prologue presents a vivid portrait of 14th-century life; among the best-known tellers of tales are the Knight, the Miller, the Man of Law, and the Wife of Bath.

☞ SAMUEL TAYLOR COLERIDGE (1772–1834, English)

He wrote only two famous poems—one of them unfinished—but what successes they were: "The Rime of the Ancient Mariner" (that's the one about the wedding guest and the albatross) and "Kubla Khan" *(In Xanadu did Kubla Khan/ A stately pleasure-dome decree).* His friend Wordsworth could have learned a useful lesson about quality versus quantity.

☞ JOHN DONNE (1572–1631, English)

The greatest of the metaphysical poets (a loose term for a group of 17th-century poets whose work investigated the world using intellect rather than intuition). His most famous line, *"No man is an Island, entire of itself,"* oft misquoted, is from a book of devotions rather than a poem.

☞ **T(HOMAS) S(TEARNS) ELIOT** (1888–1965,
   American-born, worked in England)
Author of "The Wasteland" *(April is the cruellest month)* and
"The Love Song of J. Arthur Prufrock."

☞ **THOMAS GRAY** (1717–71, English)
Gets a mention here because we all have read his *Elegy Written
in a Country Churchyard:*

> The curfew tolls the knell of parting day,
> The lowing herd wind slowly o'er the lea,
> The plowman homeward plods his weary way,
> And leaves the world to darkness and to me.

If you wrote only one poem in your life, you probably would
have been quite happy to have written that one.*

☞ **JOHN KEATS** (1795–1821, English)
Another great Romantic, he's the one who died at the intimi-
datingly young age of 26 of consumption in Rome—you can
visit his house, located near the Spanish Steps. "La Belle Dame
Sans Merci" *(O what can ail thee, knight-at-arms/ Alone and
palely loitering?)*, "Ode to a Nightingale" *(My heart aches, and
a drowsy numbness pains/ My sense, as though of hemlock I had
drunk)*, "On First Looking into Chapman's Homer" *(Much
have I travelled in the realms of gold)* and "To Autumn" *(Season
of mists and mellow fruitfulness)*.

---

* There are four poems by Gray in the *Oxford Book of English Verse*,
one of them the endearingly named *"On a Favourite Cat, Drowned
in a Tub of Gold Fishes."*

☞ **RUDYARD KIPLING** (1865–1936, English)
Prolific chronicler of the soldier's lot in South Africa and India, but best known for "If:"

> *If you can keep your head while all about you*
>   *Are losing theirs and blaming it on you...*
>   *If you can meet with Triumph and Disaster*
> *And treat those two impostors just the same...*
> *Yours is the Earth and everything that's in it,*
> *And—which is more—you'll be a Man, my son!*

☞ **JOHN MILTON** (1608–74, English)
Best known for his epic poems, *Paradise Lost* and *Paradise Regained,* which were composed in his later years while blind; *Areopagitica,* Milton's treatise on censorship, also earned him recognition.

☞ **PERCY BYSSHE SHELLEY** (1792–1822, English)
One of the great Romantic poets, married to Mary, the author of Frankenstein. Lived mostly in Europe, latterly Italy, where he drowned in a boating accident. Author of "Ode to a Skylark" *(Hail to thee, blithe Spirit!),* "Ozymandias" *(Look on my works, ye Mighty, and despair!)* and *Adonais,* an elegy on the death of Keats.

☞ **EDMUND SPENSER** (*c.*1552–99, English)
Author of *The Faerie Queene,* an epic poem celebrating the Tudor dynasty and Elizabeth I, and known to his peers as "the prince of poets." His poem "Epithalamion" has 365 long lines,

representing the sum of 52 weeks, 12 months, and 4 seasons of the annual cycle, and 24 stanzas, corresponding to the diurnal and sidereal hours.

☞ **ALFRED LORD TENNYSON** (1809–92, English)
Another prolific one. His great work is "In Memoriam," written on the early death of his friend Arthur Hallam; but most people are probably more familiar with "Come into the Garden," "Maud," and "The Lady of Shalott":

> *Out flew the web and floated wide;*
> *The mirror crack'd from side to side;*
> *'The curse is come upon me!' cried*
> *The Lady of Shalott*

☞ **DYLAN THOMAS** (1914–53, Welsh)
Famous drunkard, but you forgive him most things for having written "Under Milkwood" and enabling Richard Burton to record it for posterity.

☞ **WILLIAM WORDSWORTH** (1770–1850, English)
The most important of the Lake Poets (the others were Coleridge and Robert Southey). I have to say, I think "prolix" rather than "prolific" is the *mot juste* for Wordsworth. He churned it out, and goodness he was dull. The often-quoted "Daffodils" (*I wander'd lonely as a cloud*) is one of his, as is the "Sonnet Written on Westminster Bridge" (*Earth hath not anything to show more fair*).

48   LITERATURE

☞ **W(ILLIAM) B(UTLER) YEATS** (1865–1939, Irish)
Theosophist and Rosicrucian as well as poet and playwright;
dedicated his early poems to Maud Gonne. Best known are
"The Song of Wandering Aengus" and "The Lake Isle of
Innisfree" *(I will arise and go now, and go to Innisfree).*

North American Poets

Although this is an extremely short list of extraordinary poets,
the writers listed here captured the voice and history of their
generations. Hopefully they will inspire you to seek out the
many remarkable poets that followed in their footsteps.

☞ **ANNE BRADSTREET** (1612–72)
A puritan, she immigrated with her family in 1630 to the New
World. Anne, who was used to an Earl's manor, had to adjust to
near-primitive living conditions. She struggled to take care of
her home and raise eight children but still found time to write
and became the first female writer to publish work in colonial
America. Some notable poems include "The Prologue" and
"To My Dear and Loving Husband."

☞ **EMILY DICKINSON** (1830–1886)
Dickinson spent a large part of her 55 years writing about
death and immortality. After all, her home overlooked the
Amherst, Massachusetts, burial ground, and since Emily was
a bit of a recluse and spent a large part of her adult life caring
for her ailing mother, she had plenty of time to contemplate
life and death through her window. Fewer than a dozen of

her poems were actually published during her lifetime. Some of her well-known poems include "Because I could not stop for Death," "Success is counted sweetest," and "A wounded deer"—leaps highest, which contains the line *Mirth is the mail of Anguish.*

☞ **ROBERT FROST** (1874–1963, American)
Probably second only to Whitman as "the great American poet," Frost won the Pulitzer Prize three times. His works include "Stopping by Woods on a Snowy Evening" *(And miles to go before I sleep)* and "The Road Not Taken" *(Two roads diverged in a wood, and I—/I took the one less traveled by).*

☞ **HENRY WADSWORTH LONGFELLOW** (1807–1882)
He is known for his lyric poetry—"Paul Revere's Ride," "Evange-line," and "The Song of Hiawatha" *(By the shore of Gitche Gumee,* which, incidentally, is Lake Superior). Hiawatha may be the most mocked and parodied poem of all time, receiving reconstruction from agents such as Lewis Carroll ("Hiawatha's Photographing") and the producers of *Saturday Night Live.*

☞ **WALT WHITMAN** (1819–92, American)
The great American poet of the 19th century. His master-work is *Leaves of Grass,* a massive collection of short poems, including "O Captain! My Captain!" and "When Lilacs Last in the Dooryard Bloom'd," both from the section "Memories of President Lincoln," inspired by the president's assassination.

International Authors

Most of us had teachers of English or general studies who encouraged us to broaden our horizons by reading some of the foreign "greats" in translation. Keeping this to a Top 10 has meant cheating a bit on the Greek tragedians and leaving out Horace, Ovid, Rabelais, Molière, Schiller, Balzac, Zola... and that's before I really hit the 20th century. But I think these are the ones you are most likely to have read without knowing the original language.

☞ **DANTE ALIGHIERI** (1265–1321, Italian)

Known for *The Divine Comedy,* Dante divided his epic into three parts: *Inferno* (Hell), *Purgatoria,* and *Paradiso.* It narrates Dante's journey through these three worlds, the first two guided by Virgil, the final by Beatrice, a woman with whom he had been madly in love since he was nine, although it seems they met only twice. Hell is depicted as having various circles, indicating degrees of suffering, depending on how bad you had been in life: the ninth and worst contained the poets.

☞ **MIGUEL DE CERVANTES** (1547–1616, Spanish)

One of the most influential works of Spanish literature is Cervantes's *Don Quixote.* The novel is about a man who becomes obsessed with books on chivalry and decides to go out into the world to do noble deeds. Toward this end, he imagines that a local village girl is the glamorous lady in whose name these deeds will be carried out, and he christens her Dulcinea del Toboso. His steed is actually a broken-down old horse called Rosinante, which means "previously a broken-down old horse." Along with other foolish whims, he adopts Sancho Panza as his squire and goes around attacking windmills because he thinks they are giants.

☞ FYODOR DOSTOEVSKY (1821–81, Russian)

Often credited as a founder of 20th-century existentialism, Dostoevsky graduated as a military engineer. However, he soon resigned that career, began writing, and joined a group of utopian socialists. He was arrested and sentenced to death, but the punishment was commuted and he spent eight years in hard labor and as a soldier. His best-known works include *Crime and Punishment,* an account of an individual's fall and redemption, *The Brothers Karamazov,* a tale of four brothers involved in their father's brutal murder.

☞ GUSTAV FLAUBERT (1821–80, French)

One of the most important novels of the 19th century, *Madame Bovary* was attacked for its obscenity when it was published more than 150 years ago. The novel focuses on Madame Bovary—Emma—who is married to a worthy but dull provincial doctor, Charles. She longs for glamour and passion and has adulterous affairs, rebelling against the accepted ideas of the day. The novel served to inspire the beginnings of feminism.

☞ JOHANN WOLFGANG VON GOETHE
(1749–1832, German)

Once called "Germany's greatest man of letters," Goethe is best known for his two-part drama *Faust,* the tragic play about a

man who sells his soul to the devil—here called Mephistoph-
eles—in return for worldly success. Surprisingly, he is saved
by angels. Christopher Marlowe's play *Doctor Faustus* was
the inspiration for Goethe's work. Goethe's influence spread,
extending across Europe, becoming a major source of inspiration in music, drama, poetry, and philosophy.

☞ **HOMER** (*c.* 9th century B.C., Greek)
The great epics the *Iliad* and the *Odyssey* are the basis of pretty
much everything we know about the Trojan War and about
Odysseus (Ulysses)'s 10-year journey to get home to Ithaca.
A quick rundown on the Trojan War: Paris, prince of Troy,
abducted Helen, the beautiful wife of Menelaus, who was the
King of Sparta (in Greece). Various Greek heroes—Odysseus,
Achilles, Agamemnon—were pledged to fight to bring her
back. They laid siege to Troy for 10 years before finally hitting
on the idea of a wooden horse: Soldiers hid inside it, the
Trojans were fooled into taking it within the city walls, the
soldiers leaped out, and the Trojans were defeated. The Trojan
hero was Paris's older brother, Hector. Their parents were
Priam and Hecuba, and their sister Cassandra was the one
who made prophecies that no one believed. Then Odysseus set
off for home, encountering Circe, Calypso, and the Cyclops
Polyphemus on the way. Back home his wife, Penelope, had
promised her suitors that she would marry one of them when
she had finished the piece of weaving she was doing, but she
secretly unraveled the day's work every night.

☞ VICTOR HUGO (1802–85, French)

One of the most notable French Romantic writers, Hugo created his own version of the historical novel by combining historical fact with vivid, imaginative details. His great achievements were *Notre-Dame de Paris,* known to us as *The Hunchback of Notre-Dame,* and *Les Miserables.* The hunchback Quasimodo is the bell ringer at Notre-Dame, and the plot concerns his love for the Gypsy girl Esmeralda. *Les Miserables,* known to many because of its successful stage adaptations, is set in Paris in 1815, at the time of the Battle of Waterloo. The central character, Jean Valjean, is a reformed thief who is persecuted by the police agent Javert.

☞ SOPHOCLES (*c.* 496–406 B.C., Greek); EURIPIDES (*c.* 480–406 B.C.); ARISTOPHANES (*c.* 448–380 B.C.)

Oedipus Rex, also known as *Oedipus the King,* is the play about the man who accidentally married his mother. It is the first in Sophicles's *Oedipus* Trilogy, followed by *Oedipus at Colonus* and then *Antigone. Medea,* the play about the woman who murdered her children to avenge herself on their father is by **Euripides**, who lived around the same time. And while we're at it, there was the comic playwright **Aristophanes**, who wrote *Lysistrata,* about the women who put a stop to the Peloponnesian War by refusing to have sex with their husbands.

☞ **LEO TOLSTOY** (1828–1910, Russian)

Born into Russian nobility and widely regarded by fellow writers as one of the world's greatest novelists, Tolstoy is best known for his epic, *War and Peace*. A rich tale of early 19th century czarist Russia under Alexander I, it discusses the absurdity and shallowness of war and aristocratic society. Tolstoy's *Anna Karenina* is the book he considered to be his first novel. Considered a true example of realist fiction, it centers on adultery and self-discovery while social changes storm through Russia.

☞ **VIRGIL** (70–19 B.C., Roman)

His most famous work is *The Aeneid,* the story of the Trojan prince Aeneas, the ancestor of the Roman people (also an ancestor of Romulus and Remus, who actually founded the city). Some of *The Aeneid* was inspired by Homer and relates to the story of the fall of Troy. Escaping from Troy, Aeneas eventually reached Italy but stopped off en route in Carthage, where he had an affair with the queen, Dido, who burned herself alive when he left her. The first words of the *Aeneid* are *"Arma virumque cano"*—*"I sing of arms and the man"*—which is where the title of George Bernard Shaw's play comes from.

MATH

Remember when you used to harangue your parents about why you needed to know "this stuff"? It was only later that you found out why as you wrestled with the challenges of chemistry, engineering, physics, architecture or more ordinary kinds of problems such as figuring your income tax and balancing your checkbook. That math you found so useless as a child is not so useless after all, is it? But perhaps over the years you have found yourself floundering for some of those rules and answers you might have known if you hadn't been doodling on your notebook during class. Well, flounder no more....

Arithmetic

Arithmetic is all about sums—adding, subtracting, multiplying, and dividing—each with its own vocabulary:

- If you add two or more numbers together, their total is a **sum**. So 7 is the sum of 4 + 3.
- With subtraction you find the **difference** between two numbers. The difference between 9 and 7 is the smaller number subtracted from the larger: 9 – 7, and the difference is 2.
- If you multiply two or more numbers together, the answer is a **product**. So 30 is the product of 6 x 5.
- With division you divide a **divisor** into a **dividend** and the answer is a **quotient**. If there is anything left over, it is called a **remainder**. So 15 divided by 2 gives a quotient of 7 with a remainder of 1.

☞ LONG MULTIPLICATION

If you are old enough to have taken math exams without the aid of a calculator, you will have learned the times tables. The easiest one is the 11 times table because it goes 11, 22, 33, 44, and so on—but it all goes a bit wrong after 99. Many people learn by rote up to 12 x 12 = 144; beyond that a person really needs to understand what they are doing. For example:

$$\begin{array}{r} 147 \\ \times\ \ 63. \\ \hline \end{array}$$

After the number 9, you have to use two digits. The right-hand digit in any whole number represents the units; to the left are the tens and then the hundreds and so on. So 63 is made up of 6 tens, or 60, plus 3 units. And in this problem, you need to multiply 147 by each of those elements separately.

Start from the right: 3 x 7 = 21, so you write down the 1 and "carry" the 2 to the next column;

3 x 4 = 12, plus the 2 you have carried = 14. Write down the 4 and carry the 1;

3 x 1 = 3, plus the 1 you carried = 4.

So 3 x 147 = 441.

To multiply 147 by 60, put a 0 in the right-hand column and multiply by 6 (because any number multiplied by 10 or a multiple of 10 ends in 0);

6 x 7 = 42, so write down the 2 and carry 4;

6 x 4 = 24, plus the 4 you have carried = 28. Write down the 8 and carry 2;

6 x 1 = 6, plus the 2 you have carried = 8.

So 60 x 147 = 8,820;

63 x 147 is therefore the sum of 60 x 147 (8,820) and 3 x 147 (441), which equals 9,261.

Or

$$
\begin{array}{r}
147 \\
\times\ 63 \\
\hline
441 \\
8820 \\
\hline
9261.
\end{array}
$$

Songwriter and mathematician Tom Lehrer plays a tune about New Math, in which he does his problem in base 8. If you do a search on Youtube.com for Lehrer's New Math, you'll see why this section avoids that technique.

☞ LONG DIVISION

Division is multiplication in reverse, so start with 9,261 and divide it by 63.

If you have a divisor of 12 or less, the times tables does or did the work for you: You *know* or knew that 72 divided by 8 was 9, without having to work it out. But with a number larger than 12, you need to be more scientific:

$$
63\overline{)\,9261.}
$$

With division you work through the number from left to right.

You can't divide 63 into 9, for the simple reason that 63 is larger than 9. So look at the next column. You *can* divide 63 into 92—once—so you write a 1 at the top of the sum. But it doesn't go into 92 once exactly—there is a remainder, which is the difference between 92 and 63; in other words, 92 minus 63, which is 29.

Carry 29 forward into the next column and put it in front of the 6 to give you 296. Does 63 go into 296? Yes, it must, because 296 is bigger than 63, but how many times? Well, look at the left-hand figures of the two numbers and you'll see something that you can solve using the times table: 6 into 29. That's easy: Four 6s are 24, so 6 goes into 29 four times, with a bit left over. So it's likely that 63 will go into 296 four times with a bit left over. Indeed 4 x 63 = 252, and the bit left over is 296 minus 252, which equals 44.

Write 4 at the top of the sum, next to the 1, and carry 44 forward into the next column to make 441. How many times does 63 go into 441? Well, 6 goes into 44 seven times (6 x 7 = 42), so let's try that. And, conveniently, 63 x 7 = 441. Which means that 63 goes into 441 exactly seven times, with nothing left over, and that answers the problem: 147.

Fractions, Decimals, and Percentages

☞ PROPER FRACTIONS
A **fraction** is technically any form of number that is not a whole number; what most people think of as fractions— numbers such as ½, ⅔, ¾, and so on—are properly called vulgar, simple, or common fractions (as opposed to decimal fractions; see page 60).

The top number in these fractions is called the **numerator**, the bottom one the **denominator** (remember, **d**enominator **d**own).

In fact, the examples given above are all **proper** fractions, with the numerator smaller than the denominator (the fraction represents less than 1). In an **improper** fraction the reverse is true, as in ²²⁄₇ (an approximation for pi, see page 73), which can also be written as 3¹⁄₇, because 7 goes into 22 three times, with a remainder of 1.

If you want to solve problems that involve fractions, it is important to know that if you divide or multiply both the numerator and denominator by the same number, you produce a fraction that is the same value as the original fraction. Take ½. Multiply both numerator and denominator by 2 and you get ²⁄₄. Which is still a half, because 2 is half of 4. Or multiply ½ by 3 and you get ³⁄₆. Which again is still a half, because 3 is half of 6.

The same principle applies to division: If you start with ³⁄₆ and divide top and bottom by 3, you reduce your fraction down to ½ again. This process is called canceling. When you can't cancel anymore, the fraction is in its lowest terms.

With addition and subtraction, however, you can only add and subtract fractions that have the same denominator. You can add ½ + ½ and get ²⁄₂, which equals 1, because two halves make a whole. But what you have done is add the two numerators together. The denominator stays the same, because you are adding like to like. (It's no different from adding 1 apple to 1 apple to get 2 apples.)

Now say you want to add ½ + ⅓. It's easy to do, but first you must convert them so they have the same denominator. The lowest common denominator of 2 and 3 (the smallest number into which both will divide) is 6. To turn ½ into sixths, you need to multiply both parts of the fraction by 3:

$$\frac{1 \times 3}{2 \times 3} = \frac{3}{6}\ .$$

So ½ is the same thing as ³⁄₆.

To convert ⅓ into sixths, you need to multiply both parts by 2:

$$\frac{1 \times 2}{3 \times 2} = \frac{2}{6}\ .$$

So ⅓ is the same thing as ²⁄₆.

Now you have something that you can add, on the same principle of adding the numerators together:

$$\tfrac{3}{6} + \tfrac{2}{6} = \tfrac{5}{6}\ .$$

The same applies to subtraction:

$$\tfrac{7}{10} - \tfrac{3}{10} = \tfrac{4}{10}\ .$$

But both 4 and 10 can be divided by 2, to give the simpler fraction ⅖.

☞ DECIMAL FRACTIONS

The word decimal refers to anything *with the number 10,* and the English system is based on multiples of 10. As previously mentioned in the multiplication section, a single-digit number—say, 6—means that you have six units of whatever it is. When you have more than nine, you have to use two digits, with one digit representing the tens on the left and one digit representing the units on the right.

Decimal fractions work on the same principle, except that they go from right to left. The fraction is separated from the whole number by a dot called a **decimal point.** The figure immediately to the right of it represents tenths, to the right of that is hundredths, and so on. So 1.1 (pronounced one point one) = 1 plus one tenth of 1; 1.2 = 1 + $\frac{2}{10}$ (or $\frac{1}{5}$); 1.25 (pronounced one point two five) = 1 + $\frac{2}{100}$ + $\frac{5}{100}$, or 1 + $\frac{25}{100}$.

An interesting example is 1.25, because it is the same as 1¼. How do we know that? Well, return to the idea of dividing numerators and denominators by the same thing. For example, $\frac{25}{100}$ can be divided by 5 to give $\frac{5}{20}$. But 5 and 20 are both also divisible by 5, giving ¼. (Once you've got your numerator down to 1, you know that you have simplified the fraction as far as it will go.) So 1.25 is exactly the same as 1¼.

Decimal fractions that are less than 1 can be written either 0.25 or just .25—it's the same thing.

☞ **RECURRING DECIMALS**

Not everything divides neatly into tens, so sometimes a decimal fraction can be no more than an approximation. For example, ⅓ is 0.333 recurring—no matter how many threes you add, you will never get a decimal that is exactly equal to one third.

If a decimal recurs, you can be certain that it's the same as some common fraction. For example, 0.222 recurring is $\frac{2}{9}$;

0.142857142857142857 recurring is ⅐. A recurring decimal is sometimes indicated with a dot above the last digit, which is sort of the equivalent of ellipses (…) or "etc., etc., etc."

Pi is different (see page 73). Its decimal expansion goes on forever but without recurring, because it isn't the same as any common fraction. Pi is called a **transcendental** number, and it's probably the only one you'll ever meet.

☞ PERCENTAGES
Percent means *by a hundred*, so anything expressed as a percentage is a fraction (or part, if you prefer) of 100. So 25 percent is twenty-five parts of 100, or ²⁵⁄₁₀₀ or 0.25. If you've been paying attention, you'll know that this is the same as ¼.

Similarly, 50 percent is ⁵⁰⁄₁₀₀, which can be canceled down to ²⁵/₅₀, which is ⁵⁄₁₀, which is ½.

Mean, Median, and Mode

In arithmetical terms, **mean** is simply a fancy word for **average**. You calculate a mean by adding a group of numbers together and dividing by the number of numbers. (Strictly speaking, this is the **arithmetic mean**—there are other sorts of mean, too, but of interest only to mathematicians.) So the mean of 4, 8, 12, and 16 is the total of the four numbers, divided by 4:

$$4 + 8 + 12 + 16 = 40 \text{ divided by } 4 = 10.$$

And it works for any number of numbers. For example, if a class of 11 children gets the following marks on an exam—55, 57, 57, 65, 66, 69, 70, 72, 75, 79, and 83—the total of the marks is 748. Divide that by 11, and you get a mean of 68.

The **median** of a set of values is literally the middle one. In the set of grades above, it is 69. There are five marks lower than 69 and five marks higher than 69—never mind their actual values. The median of an even number of values is the average of the middle two. For example, the median of 1, 4, 9, 16, 25, and 36 is 12.5—halfway between 9 and 16.

The **mode** of a set of values is the most common value. The mode of our set of marks is 57, because it is the only one that occurs more than once.

Measurements

Metric units and imperial (or what we will refer to as American) units are two different ways to measure the same things. Just as Fahrenheit and Celsius both measure temperature but in different ways (see page 94), so the metric system and system of American units quantify length, weight, and all sorts of other things, using different units. Metric units are also sometimes called SI units, which stands for Système Internationale.

The metric system calculates in tens or multiples of tens. The system of American units doesn't, and to the uninitiated it can seem pretty random. (American units used to mean something sensible, such as the foot was the length of a man's foot and the yard was the distance from his nose to the tip of his outstretched arm.)

☞ LENGTH

In American units length is measured in inches, feet, yards, and miles, and occasionally also in chains and furlongs. There are 12 inches in a foot, 3 feet (36 inches) in a yard, 22 yards in a chain, 10 chains in a furlong, and 8 furlongs (1,760 yards, 5,280 feet) in a mile. Other units are still in use for some special purposes, such as the fathom (6 feet) for measuring the depth of the sea, and the hand (4 inches) for measuring the height of a horse.

The basic unit of length in the metric system is the meter, with subdivisions and multiples for measuring little things and big things. Most commonly used are the millimeter (a thousandth of a meter), the centimeter (a hundredth of a meter, or ten millimeters), and the kilometer (a thousand meters).

To convert between the two:
- 1 inch = 2.54 centimeters, so to convert inches to centimeters, multiply by 2.54. To convert centimeters to inches, divide by 2.54. Remember that a centimeter is shorter than an inch, so you should have a larger number of centimeters.
- 1 yard = 0.91 meters; 1 meter = 1.09 yards, or 3.3 feet. Yards and feet are shorter than meters, so you will have a larger number of them.
- 1 mile = 1.6 kilometers; 1 kilometer = 0.625 (⅝) of a mile. This time the metric unit is smaller, so you have more kilometers than miles.
- A nautical mile is about 1.15 miles, or *exactly* 1,852 meters.

☞ WEIGHT

In American units weight is measured in ounces, pounds, a hundredweight (short), and tons: 16 ounces (oz.) = 1 pound (lb., from *libra,* Latin for pound); 100 pounds = 1 hundredweight (short); 200 hundredweight (2,000 lb.) = 1 ton. This is sometimes called a short ton, because the imperial system in the U.K. uses a long ton of 2,240 lb. And they also use a measurement of stones (14 pounds = 1 stone).

In the metric system weight is measured in grams or kilograms. (You can have milligrams and centigrams, but a gram is already pretty small, so unless you're a pharmacist or something of that sort, you don't often need them.) A kilogram is 1,000 grams.

- 1 gram (or g) = about 0.0353 ounce, so to convert grams to ounces, multiply the number of grams by .0353. To convert ounces to grams, divide by .0353.
- 1 kilogram (or kilo or kg) is about 2.2 pounds, so multiply kilograms by 2.2, divide pounds by 2.2.
- A metric ton is 1,000 kilograms, or 2,205 pounds, just a bit more than an American ton.

☞ VOLUME

In the American system volume is measured in fluid ounces, pints, quarts, and gallons; in the metric system it is measured in liters. This becomes even more complicated because the value of the units in the United States differs from the imperial system in the U.K.

In the United States 16 fluid ounces make a pint. But the U.S. pint and gallon are smaller than the U.K. ones. To convert U.S. pints to liters, divide by 2.1.

In the U.K. 20 imperial fluid ounces make 1 imperial pint, 2 imperial pints make 1 imperial quart, and there are 4 quarts (8 pints) in an imperial gallon. A liter is about 1.75 pints, so to convert imperial pints to liters, divide by 1.75; to convert liters to imperial pints, multiply by 1.75 (pints are smaller, so you will have more of them).

Algebra and Equations

Algebra is the branch of math that uses symbols (normally letters of the alphabet) to represent unknown numbers, along the lines of $a + b = 5$. If you assign a value to a, you can calculate b: If $a = 2$, then $b = 3$. This is known as an **algebraic equation**.

The main thing to remember when solving equations is that one side of the = sign is equal to the other side, so anything that you do to one side, you need to do to the other.*

For example, to solve the equation

$$3a + 1 = 16 - 2a,$$

you first add $2a$ to each side, giving:

$$5a + 1 = 16.$$

Then subtract 1 from each side, giving

$$5a = 15.$$

Now you can divide both sides by 5 and announce proudly that $a = 3$.

☞ SIMULTANEOUS EQUATIONS

A simultaneous equation is a more complicated form of

---

*You're allowed to do almost anything to an equation, as long as you do the same thing to both sides. You are not allowed, however, to a) take square roots; or b) divide by 0. You wouldn't normally divide anything by 0 anyway, but if you were to divide something by, say, a–3 and it turned out that a equaled 3, you would get some very odd answers. More on square roots later in this section.

algebraic equation, in which you have two or more unknowns. The general rule is that you must have exactly the same number of equations as you have unknowns in order to find the value of each. If you have fewer equations, there will be lots of solutions and no way to choose between them. If you have too many equations, there will be no solution at all.

This assumes that the equations are all different and don't contradict each other. For example:

$$a + b = 6,$$
$$2a + 2b = 12$$

are no good as a pair of simultaneous equations, because they both say exactly the same thing, while:

$$a + b = 6,$$
$$a + b = 7$$

will not work either, because there's no way both of them can be true at the same time.

Here's a look at a better-behaved set of simultaneous equations:

$$a+b = 6,$$
$$a-b = 2.$$

A way of solving these is to add the two equations together, so

$$a + a + b - b = 6+2$$

or, more simply, $2a = 8$ (because the $+b$ and $-b$ cancel each other out).

From there you can calculate that $a = 4$ and, because $a + b = 6$, b must equal 2. Which is verified by the second equation, $4 - 2 = 2$.

The principle remains the same regardless of how many unknowns you have:

$$a + b + c = 24,$$
$$a + b - c = 16,$$
$$2a + b = 32.$$

Add the first two equations together and you get $2a + 2b = 40$ (because this time the c's cancel each other out).

Now look at the third equation. It's very similar to the sum of the first two. Subtract one from the other:

$$(2a + 2b) - (2a - b) = 40 - 32.$$

The a's cancel each other out, so $2b - b$ (in other words, b) $= 8$.

Go back to the third equation, which contains only a's and b's, and substitute 8 for b:

$$2a + 8 = 32.$$

Deduct 8 from each side of the equation to give

$$2a = 32 - 8 = 24,$$

which means that $a = 12$.

Now go back to the first equation and substitute both a and b:

$$12 + 8 + c = 24,$$
$$20 + c = 24,$$
$$c = 24 - 20 = 4.$$

Verify this by going to the second equation:

$$12[a] + 8[b] - 4[c] = 16,$$

which is true.

☞ QUADRATIC EQUATIONS

These are more complex again, because they involve a square—that is, a number multiplied by itself and written with a raised ^{2} after it—so 16 is 4^2, and 36 is 6^2. Thus, 4 is the square root of 16, and 6 is the square root of 36. The symbol for a **square root** is $\sqrt{}$. Actually, $(-4)^2$ is also 16, so 16 has two square roots: +4 and -4. Any positive number has two square roots. A negative number doesn't have any square roots at all, because if you multiply a negative by a negative, you get a positive.

An algebraic expression can also be a square: the square of $a + 4$ is $(a + 4)$ x $(a + 4)$. You do this by multiplying each of the elements in the first bracket by each of the elements in the second:

$$(a \times a) + (a \times 4) + (4 \times a) + (4 \times 4)$$
$$= a^2 + 8a + 16.$$

To solve a quadratic equation, you need to turn both sides of it into a perfect square, which is easier to explain if we look at an example:

$$a^2 + 8a = 48.$$

The rule for "completing the square" in order to solve a quadratic equation is, "Take the number before the a, square it, and divide by 4." For example, 8 squared (64) divided by 4 is 16, so we add that to both sides; reassuringly, we already know that adding 16 to this equation will create a perfect square, because we just did it in the previous equation:

$$a^2 + 8a + 16 = 48 + 16 = 64.$$

Taking the square root of each side gives:

$$a + 4 = 8 \text{ (because 8 is the square root of 64).}$$

Again, we know that $a + 4$ is the square root of $a^2 + 8a + 16$, because it was part of the sum we did on the previous page. Anyway, we now have a simple sum to establish that $a = 4$.

Wait a minute, though. Taking the square root of both sides of an equation is not allowed. Why is this? Because a positive number like 64 has *two* square roots, +8 and –8. So the truth of the matter is that actually

$$a + 4 = +8 \text{ or } -8,$$

so a equals either +4 or –12.

Although this example is an easy one, the beauty of algebra is that the same principle applies whatever the numbers involved. So, to repeat: The rule for "completing the square" in order to solve a quadratic equation is, Take the number before the a, square it, and divide by 4.)

So if your equation is

$$a^2 + 12a + 14 = 33,$$

you first simplify the equation by getting rid of the 14. Subtract it from both sides to leave:

$$a^2 + 12a = 33 - 14 = 19.$$

Square the 12 to give 144, divide by 4 to give 36, and—as always—add that to both sides:

$$a^2 + 12a + 36 = 19 + 36 = 55.$$

The square root of that gives you

$$a + 6 = 55 = (approximately)\ 7.4,\ or,\ of\ course,\ -7.4.$$

Deduct 6 from each side to leave the simple statement $a = 1.4$ or -13.4.

You can check that this is right by going back to the original equation and putting in $a = 1.4$:

$$a^2 + 12a + 14 = 33$$
$$becomes$$
$$(1.4 \times 1.4) + (12 \times 1.4) + 14 = 1.96 + 16.8 + 14$$
$$(near\ enough\ for\ the\ purposes\ of\ this\ exercise)$$
$$= 2 + 17 + 14 = 33.$$

QED, as they say in math (or essentially, problem solved). You'll find it also works out with $a = -13.4$.

Geometry

Geometry is about measuring lines and angles and assessing the relationship between them, so let's start with some ways of measuring.

- The **perimeter** of a two-dimensional object is the total length of all its sides. For example, if these sides are straight, it's a matter of simple addition: A rectangle measuring 4 inches by 5 inches has two sides 4 inches long and two sides 5 inches long, so its perimeter is 4 + 5 + 4 + 5 = 18 inches.
- The **area** of a four-sided figure is calculated by multiplying the length by the width: In the above example 4 x 5 = 20 square inches (in.^{2}).
- **Volume** is calculated in the same way, by multiplying the length by the width by the height (or, if you prefer, the area by the height). For instance, a box that is 6 inches high, whose base measures 4 inches by 5 inches, has a volume of 4 x 5 x 6 = 120 cubed inches (in^3).

The volume of a pyramid is the area of the base multiplied by the height, divided by 3:

$$\frac{h \times b}{3}.$$

It's when you get to circles that it all becomes more complicated, because then you have to start dealing with…

☞ PI

Pi (π) is the Greek equivalent of the Roman *p* and is used in math to represent the ratio of the circumference of a circle to its diameter. Depending on how sophisticated you are as a mathematician, you can say that π = 3.142, 3.14159, or 3.14159265358979323846426433832795, but even then it is not 100 percent exact. Expressed as a fraction, pi is roughly 3$\frac{1}{7}$, or $\frac{22}{7}$.

Before we go on, three more quick definitions:
- The **circumference** of a circle is its perimeter, the distance around the outside.
- The **diameter** is the length of a straight line through the middle, from one point on the circumference to another.
- The **radius** is half the diameter; that is, the distance from the center of the circle to the circumference.

So to calculate the circumference of a circle, you multiply the diameter by π: a circle that is, say, 7 inches in diameter has a circumference of 7 x $\frac{22}{7}$ = approximately 22 inches. The formula for this can be expressed as πd, but is usually given as 2(πr).

Area is πr²—that is, π times the radius squared. So a circle of 6 inches radius has an area of $\frac{22}{7}$ x (6 x 6) = approximately 113 square inches.

The three-dimensional equivalent to a circle is a **sphere**, and its volume is calculated by the formula $\frac{4}{3}$πr³—that is, four thirds (or one and one third) of the product of π and the radius cubed (multiplied by itself and then by itself again). So a sphere with a radius of 6 inches has a volume of $\frac{4}{3}$ x π x(6 x 6 x 6) = approximately 905 cubic inches.

A **cone** is effectively a pyramid with a circular base, so the pyramid formula applies: A cone with a base 6 inches in diameter and a height of 10 inches has a base area of π x (6 x 6) = approximately 113 square inches, and a volume of:

$$\frac{10 \times 113}{3}$$

or

$$\frac{1130}{3},$$

which equals approximately 377 cubic inches.

☞ **TRIANGLES**

The area of a triangle is calculated by:

$$\frac{base \times height}{2}.$$

There are three types of triangles, depending on the length of their sides:

- An **equilateral** triangle has three sides of equal length.
- An **isosceles** triangle has two sides of equal length.
- A **scalene** triangle has three sides that are all of different lengths.

The sum total of the angles of a triangle, whatever its shape, is 180°. A **right angle** is 90°; any angle smaller than 90° is called an **acute angle,** while anything above 90° but lower than 180° is **obtuse.** In a right-angled triangle the side opposite the right

angle (also always the longest side) is called the **hypotenuse,**
which brings us neatly to…

☞ THE PYTHAGOREAN THEOREM

This theorem states that the square on the hypotenuse is equal
to the sum of the squares on the other two sides. The simplest
example of this is what is called a 3:4:5 triangle, in which the
hypotenuse is 5 inches (or centimeters or miles, it doesn't
matter) and the other two sides are 3 inches and 4 inches.

The square on the side that is 3 inches long is 9 in.^{2} (3 x 3),
the square on the 4-inch side is 16 in.^{2} (4 x 4), and when you
add them together, you get 25 in.^{2}, which is the square of the
hypotenuse (5 x 5).

This can also be remembered using the formula $a^2 + b^2 = c^2$,
where c is the hypotenuse.

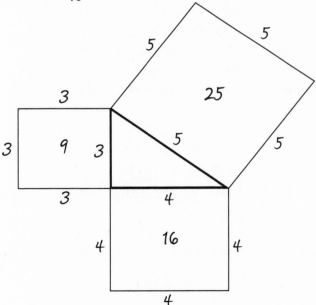

The burning question, of course, is, Why does it matter? Well, it *could* have had some practical value in the ancient world. It has been suggested, for example, that the Egyptians could have used ropes in the proportion 3:4:5 to produce right angles when building the pyramids. Unfortunately, there isn't the remotest scrap of evidence that they did any such thing. In fact, the Pythagorean theorem matters most to mathematicians because it is fundamental to our next topic.

Trigonometry

Trigonometry is "the branch of mathematics that deals with the relations between the sides and angles of a triangle," and a **trigonometric function** is "any function of an angle that is defined by the relationship between the sides and angles of a right-angled triangle."

There are six basic trigonometric functions: sine, cosine, tangent, cotangent, secant, and cosecant, and they are calculated as follows. In a right-angled triangle where the other two angles are valued at x and y degrees, the side opposite x is a, the side opposite y is b, and the hypotenuse is c:

$$\sin x = a/c$$
$$\cos x = b/c$$
$$\tan x = a/b$$
$$\cot x = b/a$$
$$\sec x = c/b$$
$$\operatorname{cosec} x = c/a$$

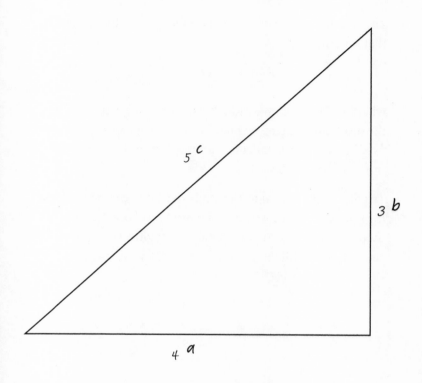

Why do we care? Well, the point is that the functions or ratios remain the same whatever the size of the triangle. So if you know the sine of a 45° angle in a triangle whose sides measure 3, 4, and 5 inches, you can extrapolate all sorts of measurements for a much larger triangle with the same proportions.

The trigonometric version of the Pythagorean theorem tells us that for any angle x,

$$sin^2x + cos^2x = 1,$$

where $\sin^2 x$ is a conventional way of writing $(\sin x)^2$ without the need for brackets. If you know the sine of an angle, you can use this formula to calculate all the rest of the trigonometric functions given above.

Trigonometry is vital to the study of higher mathematics and the sciences. At a more comprehensible and practical level, it is used in land surveying, mapmaking, engineering, astronomy, geography, satellite navigation systems, and so on.

SCIENCE

The world of science is so vast and expanding that to condense it into 30 pages seems like a futile experiment. Every school system teaches the topic differently, so what may seem familiar and commonplace to one person can remain a mystery to others. Consider this chapter the foundation on which you can build.

Biology

The term biology comes from the Greek, meaning *study of life;* therefore, this field of learning concerns plants and animals and how the human body works.

☞ PHOTOSYNTHESIS

This is the process by which plants convert carbon dioxide and water into the carbohydrates they need for growth, using energy that they absorb from light (hence, the photo element). Light is absorbed into the plant by the green pigment called chlorophyll, stored mainly in the leaves, which provides the green color of so many plants. In fact, plants need only the hydrogen element from water (H_2O), so photosynthesis releases oxygen back into the atmosphere, enabling the rest of us to breathe.

☞ THE STRUCTURE OF A PLANT

The **flower** contains the plant's reproductive organs. The stigma, style, and ovary make up the carpel, which contains the female cells; if a flower has more than one carpel, these combine to form the pistil. The male organ is called the stamen and consists of an anther that contains the pollen sacs and is supported on a filament. Most plants self-pollinate, but some, such as certain hollies and the kiwifruit, require a male and female plant of the same species in order to reproduce.

The **leaves** enable the plant to feed and breathe. They contain the chlorophyll that is essential to photosynthesis, which absorbs light. Leaves also contain pores (stoma), through which gases and water are absorbed and released back into the atmosphere. The shape of the leaf reflects the plant's needs: big, broad leaves are designed to absorb maximum light; the fleshy, succulent leaves of a cactus store water in case of drought.

The **stem** is the plant's support and the conduit between roots, leaves, and plants. It contains phloem, a tissue that transports food within the plant; and xylem, which principally transports water. It is the xylem that hardens to form the trunks of trees and shrubs.

The **roots** anchor the plant in the ground and absorb nutrients and water from the soil. A tap root system has a single main root; a fibrous system has—well, lots of fibers. In root vegetables, such as turnips and carrots, the vegetable part is, in fact, a swollen root. Adventitious roots are less common; the name means *coming from the outside,* and these roots grow in unusual places, such as from the stem.

☞ THE CARBON CYCLE

The process by which carbon (in the form of carbon dioxide) is absorbed from the atmosphere during photosynthesis and is then transferred from one organism to another and eventually released back into the atmosphere is known as the carbon cycle. For example, a plant takes in carbon dioxide; the plant

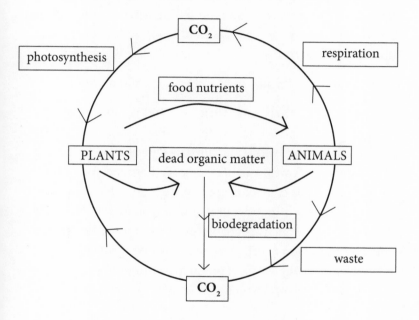

is eaten by a herbivorous animal, which is in turn eaten by a carnivore; when the animal dies, its rotting body releases carbon dioxide. Alternatively, the herbivorous animal excretes its waste, which also degrades to give off carbon dioxide.

This provides a smooth transition from plants to the human body.

☞ CHROMOSOMES

A normal human body has 46 chromosomes composed of 22 matched pairs and two sex chromosomes. Half of each pair, along with a single sex chromosome, is found in the sperm. The other half is in the egg. Fusion of the two creates the human embryo. Sex chromosomes are of two types, called X (female) and Y (male). The egg always contains an X chromosome, so the sex of the embryo is determined by whether a sperm is carrying an X or Y chromosome. Other chromosomes dictate other genetic factors, such as hair and eye color.

Chromosomes are made up of DNA, RNA, and protein.

DNA stands for deoxyribonucleic acid and is fundamental to the organization and functioning of living cells. It consists of the famous "double helix" (identified by the scientists Crick and Watson in 1953), with two strands coiled around each other. When the strands of a helix separate, each provides a template for the synthesis of an identical strand, containing the same genetic information. This enables normal growth, cell repair, and the production of cells that will turn into the next generation—which is why humans produce babies rather than tiger cubs, and why tigers produce tiger cubs rather than roses.

RNA stands for ribonucleic acid, which occurs as a single strand and contains different sugars and bases but is otherwise structurally similar to DNA. It's vital to the synthesis of…

Proteins, which fulfill many important roles in a living organism—they are involved in the makeup of tissue; the properties of muscles; and the functioning of hormones, the immune system, and the digestive system, to name a few. They are manufactured within cells using information conveyed by the DNA and RNA.

☞ THE SKELETAL SYSTEM

The human skeleton is made up of more than 200 bones, held together by fibrous tissue called **ligaments,** and linked at the **joints.** Joints allow varying degrees of movement from none (between the bones that make up the skull) through some (the hinge joints at the elbow and knee) to lots (the ball-and-socket joints at the hip and shoulder).

The principal bones of the body, starting at the top and working down, are:

- **cranium:** skull
- **spine:** made up of 26 smaller bones called vertebrae
- **clavicle:** collar bone
- **scapula:** shoulder blade
- **humerus:** upper arm
- **radius** and **ulna:** lower arm—the radius is the broader one on the thumb side, the ulna the narrower one on the little finger side
- **carpus:** a collective name for the bones of the wrist, individually known as carpals
- **metacarpus:** ditto for the five long bones of the hand
- **phalanges:** fingers
- **sacrum:** actually a fusion of five vertebrae attached to the
- **hip bone**
- **coccyx:** tail bone, a fusion of the lowest four vertebrae
- **femur:** thigh bone
- **patella:** knee cap
- **tibia** and **fibula:** lower leg—the tibia is the broader one that runs down toward the big toe; the fibula the narrower one that runs toward the little toe

- **tarsus:** a collective name for the bones of the ankle and heel, individually known as tarsals
- **metatarsus:** ditto for the five long bones of the foot
- **phalanges:** toes

☞ THE CIRCULATORY SYSTEM

Blood is the body's transportation system—everything from oxygen to hormones is transported around the body in the bloodstream, and its waste products, from carbon dioxide to urea, are carried away for disposal.

In order for blood to do its job, it needs to be pumped around, and that is the primary purpose of the **heart**. The heart is two pumps, each consisting of two chambers—an auricle and a ventricle—with a valve in between. The left side of the heart receives oxygen-rich blood from the lungs and forces it throughout the body; the right side receives the oxygen-depleted blood and returns it to the lungs to be re-oxygenated. (Oxygen, of course, comes into the lungs in the air that we breathe, and without it the cells in the body would die.)

All this requires a well-organized system of blood vessels. These are divided into **arteries,** which are strong and muscular and carry fast-flowing blood *away* from the heart, and **veins**, which are weaker and more sluggish and bring it back. The principal artery, the **aorta,** divides into smaller arteries and arterioles. Smaller veins are called venules, and really tiny blood vessels—whether veins or arteries—are called capillaries.

The exception to the useful mnemonia—*arteries go away*—is the pulmonary artery—the one that goes from the lung to the heart. The pulmonary vein runs from the heart to the lungs. Therefore, the truth is that the arteries simply carry the oxygen-rich blood.

Blood has four major components:

- **red blood cells,** which carry hemoglobin, made up of heme (an iron-containing pigment) and globin (a protein) (This combines with oxygen to form oxyhemoglobin, the means by which oxygen is transported throughout the body. Oxyhemoglobin also gives the blood its red color, which is why arterial blood is bright red; venous blood, having deposited oxygen in cells all over the body, has a bluish tinge.)
- **white blood cells,** or leukocytes, which fight infection
- **platelets,** which are necessary for the clotting process
- **plasma,** the liquid that makes the blood… well, liquid

☞ THE DIGESTIVE SYSTEM

The digestive process is divided into four parts:

- **ingestion:** eating food
- **digestion:** breaking the food down into constituent parts
- **absorption:** extracting nutrients from the food
- **elimination:** disposing of waste

Once you swallow food or drink, it enters the **esophagus,** or gullet, and passes (through a process of muscular contraction called **peristalsis**) into the stomach. From there it continues into the **small intestine** (comprising the duodenum, jejunum, and ileum), where digested food is absorbed into the bloodstream. The whole process is helped by the secretion of **enzymes**. One of the effects of the digestion of protein (which enters the body via meat, fish, eggs, etc.) is the release of **amino acids**, which are the building blocks of the protein the body needs for all sorts of different purposes.

Anything undigested after this stage passes into the **colon** (the beginning of the large intestine), where water is extracted from it. What remains are the feces, which pass through the rectum and out of the body via the anus.

Organs encountered along the way include:
- the **liver,** which in adult life often copes with our alcohol intake, but which has many more functions to do with digestion and keeping the blood healthy
- the **gall bladder,** which stores bile, needed in the digestion of fats
- the **pancreas,** which secretes various enzymes and the hormones insulin and glucagon, which regulate levels of blood sugar
- the **kidneys,** which control the amount of salt and water in the blood. (Excess fluid containing waste products is filtered through the kidneys down to the bladder and leaves the body in the form of urine.)

☞ THE RESPIRATORY SYSTEM
Air passes into the body through the **trachea** or windpipe via the mouth and nose. With the help of contractions from the **diaphragm,** which is a large muscle extending across the bottom of the rib cage, it is carried down into the lungs via two smaller tubes, called **bronchi,** which then split into even smaller bronchioles. Inside the lungs are lots of little air sacs, or **alveoli.** Within the alveoli oxygen is extracted from the air, absorbed into the bloodstream, and carried off to the heart via the pulmonary artery. The pulmonary vein brings "used" blood back to the alveoli, and the process is reversed as we breathe out air that now has a high carbon dioxide content.

☞ THE NERVOUS SYSTEM
The brain, spinal cord, and nerves make up perhaps the most

important and intricately complex system in the human body. The nervous system essentially controls all the other systems in your body. It is what allows you to remember things, or at least remember that you used to know something. It tells your muscles and organs what to do and how to do it. The three interconnected parts of the nervous system are:

- the **central nervous system,** composed of the brain and spinal cord, which sends nerve impulses and analyzes information from the sense organs (eyes, ears, nose, mouth, skin, etc.). These organs enable you to see, touch, taste, hear, and feel.

- the **peripheral nervous system,** which includes the craniospinal nerves, a vast network of nerves that extends from your brain and spinal cord to all parts of your body and carries signals back and forth. It carries nerve impulses from the central nervous system to the muscles and glands.

- the **autonomic nervous system (ANS),** which regulates involuntary actions, such as pulse rate and digestion. The ANS is broken into the sympathetic nervous system (fight or flight), the parasympathetic nervous system (rest so you can digest), and the enteric nervous system (the digestive system's personal messenger).

However, no discussion of the nervous system is complete without those trusty **neurons,** the nerve cells that send and carry the signals throughout your body. A neuron consists of a main cell body with a long nerve fiber, called an **axon,** branching from it. Electrical signals pass from axon to axon through small gaps called **synapses.** In order to do this, these electrical signals turn into chemical ones, called **neurotransmitters.** In fact, right now the neurons in the temporal lobe of your brain (which interprets language), your frontal lobe (which involves reasoning), and your occipital lobe (which controls sight) are firing away!

Chemistry

This is the study of elements and compounds and the reactions they undergo—which is a definition that surely cries out for a few more definitions.

atom: the smallest particle in an element that can take part in a chemical reaction, made up of a **nucleus,** which is containing positively charged **protons** and neutral **neutrons;** and a number of **electrons,** which are negatively charged particles that orbit the nucleus. Each atom normally has the same number of protons and electrons, leaving it with a neutral charge. The movement of electrons is responsible for most commonly observed chemical, electrical, or magnetic reactions. If an atom loses or gains an electron, it becomes either positively or negatively charged and is known as an **ion.**

element: a substance that cannot be decomposed into a simpler substance by a chemical process. Groups of elements come together to form a compound. So, for example, a combination of the element hydrogen (H) and the element oxygen (O) can form the compound water (H_2O).

mole: also known as Avogadro's number or Avogadro's constant, a mole contains the same number of particles as there are in 12 g of carbon-12 atoms—that is, 6.022×10^{23} particles.

Carbon has three naturally occurring isotopes (forms of the same substance with different numbers of neutrons), and one of these is carbon-12.

molecule: the smallest particle of a compound that can exist independently and retain its properties. So in the previous example, the smallest imaginable quantity of hydrogen and oxygen joined together in the right conditions and right proportions will still produce a molecule of water. Only when the hydrogen and oxygen are chemically separated again do they lose the properties that make them water and return to being atoms of hydrogen and oxygen.

☞ THE PERIODIC TABLE OF THE ELEMENTS

The periodic table was first devised in 1889 by the Russian chemist Dmitri Mendeleev. When putting the table together, Mendeleev realized there were gaps between some of the elements. Based on this, he predicted that some elements had yet to be discovered.

The table arranges the elements in ascending order of **atomic number** (the number of protons that each possesses) in such a way that the vertical columns contain groups or families with similar chemical properties. The horizontal rows represent periods, with the most electropositive (an alkali metal) on the left and the so-called inert gases on the right, and the whole thing proves that "the chemical properties of the elements are periodic functions of their atomic weights"—or, in other words, that similar properties in an element recur at regular intervals.

1A																	
1 **H** 1.00794 Hydrogen	2A																
3 **Li** 6.341 Lithium	4 **Be** 9.012182 Beryllium																
11 **Na** 22.989769 Sodium	12 **Mg** 24.3050 Magnesium	3B	4B	5B	6B	7B	⎴———8B———⎴										
19 **K** 39.0983 Potassium	20 **Ca** 40.078 Calcium	21 **Sc** 44.955912 Scandium	22 **Ti** 47.867 Titanium	23 **V** 50.9415 Vanadium	24 **Cr** 51.9961 Chromium	25 **Mn** 54.938045 Manganese	26 **Fe** 55.845 Iron	27 **Co** 58.933195 Cobalt	28 **Ni** 58.6934 Nickel
37 **Rb** 85.4678 Rubidium	38 **Sr** 87.62 Strontium	39 **Y** 88.90585 Yttrium	40 **Zr** 91.224 Zirconium	41 **Nb** 92.90638 Niobium	42 **Mo** 95.96 Molybdenum	43 **Tc** [98] Technetium	44 **Ru** 101.07 Ruthenium	45 **Rh** 102.90550 Rhodium	46 **Pd** 106.42 Palladium
55 **Cs** 132.9054519 Cesium	56 **Ba** 137.327 Barium	57-71 *Lanthanides	72 **Hf** 178.49 Hafnium	73 **Ta** 180.94788 Tantalum	74 **W** 183.84 Tungsten	75 **Re** 186.207 Rhenium	76 **Os** 190.23 Osmium	77 **Ir** 192.217 Iridium	78 **Pt** 195.084 Platinum
87 **Fr** [223] Francium	88 **Ra** [226] Radium	89-103 **Actinides	104 **Rf** [267] Rutherfordium	105 **Db** [268] Dubnium	106 **Sg** [271] Seaborgium	107 **Bh** [272] Bohrium	108 **Hs** [270] Hassium	109 **Mt** [276] Meitnerium	110 **Ds** [281] Darmstadtium

	57 **La** 138.90547 Lanthanum	58 **Ce** 140.116 Cerium	59 **Pr** 140.90765 Praseodymium	60 **Nd** 144.242 Neodymium	61 **Pm** [145] Promethium	62 **Sm** 150.36 Samarium	63 **Eu** 151.964 Europium
*Lanthanides							
**Actinides	89 **Ac** [227] Actinium	90 **Th** 232.03806 Thorium	91 **Pa** 231.03588 Protactinium	92 **U** 238.02891 Uranium	93 **Np** [237] Neptunium	94 **Pu** [244] Plutonium	95 **Am** [243] Americium

The elements are traditionally designated by a one-, two-, or three-letter abbreviation, as you can see in the table, and there are 118 of them. The table above lists 103; listed below them are elements 104 through 118. From 93 upward the elements don't occur naturally but have been synthesized in particle accelerators. The last few are recent achievements, and they have temporary names based on their atomic numbers. Element 117, which will be called Ununseptium, hasn't been synthesized yet, but scientists are working on it. The lanthanides and actinides are usually separated from the rest of the table, as shown above, because—unlike the other rows—they have similar properties as you read across.

							8A
							2
							He
							4.002602
							Helium

		3A	4A	5A	6A	7A	
		5	6	7	8	9	10
		B	**C**	**N**	**O**	**F**	**Ne**
		10.811	12.0107	14.0067	15.9994	18.9984032	20.1797
		Boron	Carbon	Nitrogen	Oxygen	Fluorine	Neon
		13	14	15	16	17	18
		Al	**Si**	**P**	**S**	**Cl**	**Ar**
		26.9815386	28.0855	30.973762	32.065	35.453	39.948
		Aluminum	Silicon	Phosphorus	Sulfur	Chlorine	Argon
1B	2B						
29	30	31	32	33	34	35	36
Cu	**Zn**	**Ga**	**Ge**	**As**	**Se**	**Br**	**Kr**
63.546	65.38	69.723	72.64	74.92160	78.96	79.904	83.798
Copper	Zinc	Gallium	Germanium	Arsenic	Selenium	Bromine	Krypton
47	48	49	50	51	52	53	54
Ag	**Cd**	**In**	**Sn**	**Sb**	**Te**	**I**	**Xe**
107.8682	112.411	114.818	118.710	121.760	127.60	126.90447	131.293
Silver	Cadmium	Indium	Tin	Antimony	Tellurium	Iodine	Xenon
79	80	81	82	83	84	85	86
Au	**Hg**	**Tl**	**Pb**	**Bi**	**Po**	**At**	**Rn**
196.966569	200.59	204.3833	207.2	208.98040	[209]	[210]	[222]
Gold	Mercury	Thallium	Lead	Bismuth	Polonium	Astatine	Radon
111	112	113	114	115	116	117	118
Rg	**Uub**	**Uut**	**Uuq**	**Uup**	**Uuh**	**Uus**	**Uuo**
[280]	[285]	[284]	[289]	[288]	[293]	[294]	[294]
Roentgenium	Ununbium	Ununtrium	Ununquadium	Ununpentium	Ununhexium	Ununseptium	Ununoctium

64	65	66	67	68	69	70	71
Gd	**Tb**	**Dy**	**Ho**	**Er**	**Tm**	**Yb**	**Lu**
157.25	158.92535	162.500	164.93032	167.259	168.93421	173.054	174.9668
Gadolinium	Terbium	Dysprosium	Holmium	Erbium	Thulium	Ytterbium	Lutetium
96	97	98	99	100	101	102	103
Cm	**Bk**	**Cf**	**Es**	**Fm**	**Md**	**No**	**Lr**
[247]	[247]	[251]	[252]	[257]	[258]	[259]	[262]
Curium	Berkelium	Californium	Einsteinium	Fermium	Mendelevium	Nobelium	Lawrencium

104	Rutherfordium	Rf	112	Ununbium	Uun
105	Dubnium	Db	113	Ununtrium	Uut
106	Seaborgium	Sg	114	Ununquadium	Uuq
107	Bohrium	Bh	115	Ununpentium	Uup
108	Hassium	Hs	116	Ununhexium	Uuh
109	Meitnerium	Mt	117	Ununseptium	Uus
110	Darmstadtium	Ds	118	Ununoctium	Uuo
111	Roentgenium	Rg			

☞ **ACIDS, BASES, AND SALTS**

An **acid** is a substance (often sour and corrosive) that contains hydrogen atoms that, when dissolved in water, dissociate into ions and may be replaced by metals to form a salt.

A **base** is a compound that combines with an acid to form a salt plus water. Bases that are soluble in water are called **alkalis.** Many bases are oxides (so their formula ends in O, possibly with a little number after it) or hydroxides (OH).

A **salt** is a (usually crystalline) solid compound formed from the combination of an acid and a base by the replacement of hydrogen ions in the acid by positive ions in the base.

For example, combine sulphuric acid with the base cupric oxide in the right conditions and you have copper sulphate (that lovely bright blue stuff) and water:

$$H_2SO_4 + CuO \longrightarrow CuSO_4 + H_2O.$$

In a school lab you test whether a substance is an acid or a base with litmus paper. Acids turn litmus red; bases turn it blue. Serious scientists use the **pH**—potential of hydrogen—which is measured by sensors and electrodes and such. Pure water has a pH of 7, with anything less considered acidic and anything higher alkaline. Gardeners use this as a way of testing soil; you also sometimes see the pH listed on shampoo bottles.

Another term you might remember—and one worth mentioning here—is **valency,** which means the number of atoms of hydrogen that an atom or group displaces when forming a compound. Hydrogen has a valency of 1 and oxygen a valency of 2, which is why the formula for water is H_2O and not just

HO—because you need two atoms of hydrogen to "match" one of oxygen. Copper can have either of two valencies, which is why the one mentioned a moment ago is called cupric oxide, not just copper oxide. There's also cuprous oxide, CuO_2.

☞ OXIDATION

Oxidation is a commonly quoted chemical reaction, and the most common example of it is rust. In fact, anything that reacts when it comes into contact with oxygen is being subjected to oxidation: The green coating on an old copper coin is the result of oxidation; the browning of fruit is caused by oxygen burning away at the stuff that is released when you peel off the protective skin. Rust is, strictly speaking, the oxide that forms on iron or steel. Stainless steel doesn't rust, because it is protected by a layer of chromium, which doesn't react to oxygen in the same way.

☞ DIFFUSION AND OSMOSIS

Molecules are constantly in motion and tend to move from regions where they are in higher concentration to regions where they are less concentrated—a process known as **diffusion.** Diffusion can occur in gases, in liquids, or through solids.

Osmosis is a form of diffusion that is specific to the movement of water. Water moves through a selectively permeable membrane (that is, one that lets some types of molecules through but not others) from a place where there is a higher concentration of water to one where it is lower.

In any form of diffusion, when the molecules are evenly distributed throughout a space, they have reached **equilibrium.**

☞ BOILING AND FREEZING POINTS

If the temperature is low enough, every known substance except helium becomes a solid. The temperature at which this happens is called its **freezing point.** Above its freezing point a substance is a liquid. At the other end of the scale, if the temperature is high enough, it becomes a gas, and this is called the **boiling point.**

Solid is the only state in which a substance retains its shape; a liquid assumes the shape of its container but does not necessarily fill it; a gas expands to fill the space available.

Take water, for instance. In its solid state, it is ice and retains its shape—whether ice cube, icicle, or iceberg—until the temperature rises sufficiently for it to melt and become liquid (water). If you take a tray of melted ice cubes and pour the water into a pan, it will take the shape of the container—that is, spread out to cover the bottom—but it may only come a certain distance up the side. If, however, you then turn on the heat under the pan, put a lid on it, and boil the water, it will turn into gas (steam), fill the pan completely, and probably seep out under the lid as well.

Nonscientists commonly measure temperature according to one of two scales: Celsius and Fahrenheit, both named after the people who invented them. Celsius was also once called centigrade, from the Latin for *one hundred degrees.*

The freezing point of water is 0°C, and its boiling point is 100°C. The equivalent in Fahrenheit is 32°F and 212°F. This means that the difference between freezing and boiling is 100°C and 180°F (212 − 32).

To convert Celsius to Fahrenheit, you need to divide by 100 and multiply by 180, which can also be expressed as multiplying by 1.8, or $\frac{9}{5}$. Then, because the freezing point of water is 32°F, not 0°F, you need to add 32:

$$15°C \times 1.8 = 27; \; 27 + 32 = 59°F.$$

To reverse the process, first deduct 32 from your Fahrenheit temperature, then divide by $\frac{9}{5}$ (or multiply by $\frac{5}{9}$; it's the same thing):

$$104°F - 32 = 72; \; 72 \times \frac{5}{9} = 40°C.$$

This works for any temperature above freezing.

There are two other scales used by scientists—the Réaumur and the Kelvin. According to René Antoine Ferchault de Réaumur, water freezes at 0° and boils at 80°. Kelvin is interesting because he invented the concept of absolute zero, a temperature at which particles cease to have any energy—so a scientific impossibility, although in the laboratory, scientists have achieved temperatures within a millionth of a degree of it. Absolute zero is 0°K, or –273.15°C, which is very, very cold. Imagine how much energy you would have at that temperature.

Physics

Physics deals with the properties and interactions of matter and energy, but its theories are constantly being redefined as physicists discover new things.

☞ OPTICS

Optics is all about light and there are several terms that may ring a bell.

Remember "The angle of incidence equals the angle of reflection"? You probably do. But do you remember what it means? Well, the **angle of incidence** is the angle at which light hits a surface; with **specular** (mirrorlike) reflection the light is reflected at the same angle. If the surface is rough, you get **diffuse** reflection, which means that the light bounces off in all directions.

Light may also pass through a medium—such as glass or water—and be **refracted** (change direction). This is because of the difference in the velocity with which light passes through the two different media (say, air and water), which is measured by the **refractive index**.

☞ CONDUCTION, CONVECTION, AND RADIATION

There are three ways in which heat is transferred:

Conduction can occur in solids, liquids, or gases and means (more or less) that a cool thing is warmed up by coming into contact with a hot thing. The different levels of conductivity in metals are reflected in their uses in anything from the science lab to kitchenware: Copper, for example, is highly conductive, and therefore it works well for fast cooking (although it may react with certain foods, which is why copper-bottomed pans are often lined with tin); whereas cast iron heats slowly but then cooks evenly.

Convection occurs in liquids and gases and is the basis of the principle that hot air rises. A hot liquid or gas is generally less dense than a cool one; as the hot particles rise, cooler ones rush in underneath to take their place. As the hot particles rise, they cool and come down again, and so on.

Radiation involves the energy that all objects, hot or cold, emit. It is the only one of the three that works in a vacuum and is how the sun's rays manage to warm the Earth from such a far distance away.

Heat is not the only commodity that is transferred in these ways. There is also electrical conduction, mass convection (of which evaporation is an example), and electromagnetic radiation. So, strictly speaking, you should insert the words "heat" or "therma" in front of conduction, convection, and radiation if that is what you mean.

☞ PHYSICAL LAWS

Physics is based on properties that explain what matter and energy can or can't do; without these interactions the universe would probably fall apart. From the observation of the interactions, laws were developed. Some of the physical processes and phenomena are revealed in this section. But a few definitions might help first.

Mass is the quantity of matter a body contains. Newton defined it more precisely by bringing in inertia, which is "a property of matter by which it continues in its existing state of rest or uniform motion in a straight line, unless that state is changed by an external force." All this means is that a thing will sit still until you push it.

Force is calculated by multiplying mass by acceleration and concerns producing motion in a stationary body or changing the direction of a moving one.

Velocity is speed (the dictionary says, "measure of the rate of movement," but most people call that speed) in a given direction.

Acceleration is the rate of increase in velocity.

Work is the exertion of force overcoming resistance (which might be electrical resistance, or it could be physical resistance, such as friction).

And, regardless of what anyone else may tell you, in this context a **body** is a thing. The dictionary says, "an object or substance that has three dimensions, a mass, and is distinguishable from surrounding objects."

☞ THE LAWS OF THERMODYNAMICS

Thermodynamics is the study of heat and its relationship with other forms of energy, and it is important in the study of heat engines such as gas-driven motors and gas turbines.

The other key term here is **entropy,** which is defined as "a measure of the disorder of a system." A solid has less entropy than a liquid, since the constituent particles in a solid are in a more ordered state. The flow of energy maintatins order and life. Entropy states the opposite. Entropy takes over when energy ceases.

If you have managed to follow along this far, then you are ready for the three laws of thermodynamics:

1. Energy can change from one form to another, but it can never be created or destroyed.
2. In all energy exchanges, if no energy enters or leaves the system, the potential energy of the state will be less than that of the initial state.
3. As the thermodynamic temperature of a system approaches absolute zero, its entropy approaches zero.

The British scientist and author C. P. Snow came up with a great way of remembering the three laws:

1. You cannot win (you cannot get something for nothing, because matter and energy are conserved).
2. You cannot break even (you cannot return to the same energy state, because there is always an increase in disorder).
3. You cannot get out of the game (because absolute zero is unattainable).

Moving swiftly on.

☞ THE LAWS OF CONSERVATION OF ENERGY AND MASS

The most common of these laws states that energy in a closed system cannot be created or destroyed (it's similar to the first law of thermodynamics), and nor can mass. At a more advanced level, similar laws apply to electric charge, linear momentum, and angular momentum, but most people never get that far.

☞ NEWTON'S THREE LAWS OF MOTION

1. A body remains at rest or moves with constant velocity in a straight line unless acted upon by a force.
2. The acceleration (*a*) of a body is proportional to the force (*f*) causing it: $f = ma$, where *m* is the mass of the body in question.
3. The action of a force always produces a reaction in the body, which is of equal magnitude but opposite in direction to the action.

Newton also came up with a **law of gravity,** which states that the force between two bodies is directly proportional to the product of their masses and inversely proportional to the square of the distance between them. The universal gravitational constant that makes this equation work is called *G*, and its value is 6.673×10^{-11} newton m² per kg².

However, Einstein's general theory of relativity describes gravity more accurately.

☞ EINSTEIN'S THEORIES OF RELATIVITY

Before reviewing Einstein's general theory of relativity, take a look at his *special* theory of relativity. Before Einstein—that is, until the start of the 20th century—it was believed that the speed of light relative to an observer could be calculated in the same way as the relative speed of any other two objects (such as two cars driving at different speeds). Einstein's theory is based on the assumption that the speed of light in a vacuum is a constant (186,000 miles—or 2.998×10^8 m—per second), regardless if the observer is moving or at what speed. Furthermore, he suggested that as bodies increase in speed, they increase in mass and decrease in length (relative to the observer)—although this effect became noticeable only as objects neared the speed of light.

Relative to each observer, time moves at a slower rate. All this led him to the conclusion that mass and energy are two different aspects of the same thing, which led to the famous equation

$$E = mc^2,$$

where E is energy, m is mass, and c is the velocity of light.

So, back to gravity. The special theory of relativity concerned motion in which there was no acceleration—that is, a constant speed. The general theory extended this to consider accelerated motion. According to this, gravity is a property of space and time that is "curved" by the presence of a mass. Einstein posited that the motion of the stars and planets was controlled by this curvature of space in the vicinity of matter, and that light was also bent by the gravitational field of a massive body. Subsequent experiments have shown him to be correct.

☞ ELECTRIC CURRENT

There are also a handful of laws to do with electricity. Here's one of the more familiar:

Ohm's law states that the current *(I)* flowing through an element in a circuit is directly proportional to the voltage drop or potential difference *(V)* across it: $V = IR$, where R means resistance—anything that gets in the way of the flow of current. What this means, more or less, is that the greater the resistance (measured in ohms), the greater the voltage (measured in volts) required to push the current (measured in amps) through it.

☞ EQUATIONS OF MOTION

These are basic equations that describe the motion of a body moving with constant acceleration.

A body moving with constant acceleration (a) starts with an initial velocity (u) and achieves a final velocity (v) in a time of t seconds, covering a total distance s. If you know any three of these components, you can decipher the other two.

Acceleration can be expressed as

$$a = \frac{v - u}{t} .$$

Distance traveled (s) is simply time multiplied by average speed:

$$s = t \frac{(u + v)}{2} .$$

These two equations—one for calculating acceleration and the other for calculating distance—are essentially all that is known here, but some other equations can be obtained by combining them.

For example, eliminate v from both of them. The first equation can be recast as

$$v = u + at$$

(multiply everything by t, then add u to both sides) and the second as:

$$v = \frac{2s}{t} - u$$

(multiply everything by 2, divide by t, and deduct u from both sides).

This may sound complicated, but the point is to produce an equation that defines v. Just in case you want to calculate v, you understand.... But you also now have two equations beginning "v=," so you can put them together and deduce that:

$$u + at = \frac{2s}{t} - u,$$

which, after a bit of rearranging, is equivalent to

$$s = ut + \tfrac{1}{2}at^2.$$

This looks a bit more impressive, but it's not really telling you anything new.

Similarly, you could eliminate u from each of our original equations, yielding:

$$s = vt - \tfrac{1}{2}at^2.$$

Or eliminate t from them both to show that:

$$v^2 = u^2 + 2as.$$

So, to give an example, if a body traveling at 30 m/sec (u) accelerates at 2 m/sec/sec (a) for 10 sec (t), it reaches a velocity (v):

$$v = at + u = (2 \times 10) + 30 = 50 \text{ meters per second}$$

$$s = ut + \tfrac{1}{2}at^2 = (30 \times 10) + (\tfrac{1}{2} \times 2 \times 10^2)$$
$$= 300 + 100 = 400 \text{ meters.}$$

Average speed is distance traveled (s) divided by t, which in this instance is $^{400}/_{10} = 40$ m/sec. Which sounds reasonable, because it starts at 30 and ends up at 50.

Apparently, this isn't rocket science, unless you have a rate of acceleration equal to the force of gravity, in which case you are into the realm of projectiles and ballistics, which is, um, rocket science.

HISTORY

High-school history books are typically gargantuan tomes of no fewer than 1,500 pages. You probably never covered more than 10 chapters or so, but you still had to lug those monstrous compilations onto the bus each day. Today, with history just a click away, students can quickly locate a specific historical tidbit or surf for hours (or even days) collecting information on major historical events.

With thousands of years to cover, and many choices and opinions regarding the proper texts, this chapter can only scratch the surface. But one thing most people agree upon regarding history is the importance of its study. As writer and philosopher George Santayana stressed so insightfully, "Those who cannot remember the past are condemned to repeat it."

U.S. Presidents

At the time of publication, there have been 43 presidents of the United States. What follows is a listing of some of the most notable ones, with their time in office noted following their name. (D = Democrat, R = Republican—parties that came into being around 1828 and 1854, respectively.)

George Washington (1789–97): commander-in-chief of the forces that rebelled against British rule in the 1770s, and president of the Constitutional Convention of 1787, which produced the blueprint of today's Constitution. Unanimously elected first President of the United States two years later. Probably didn't chop down a cherry tree or tell his father that he couldn't tell a lie, but the legend persists.

John Adams (1797–1801): another major figure in the War of Independence, known as the "colossus of the debate" over the Declaration of Independence. Became America's first vice president, then president after Washington's resignation.

Thomas Jefferson (1801–09): credited with drafting the Declaration of Independence and something of a polymath, with an interest in architecture, science, and gardening, to name but a few. Lived for 17 years after ceasing to be president and became a respected elder statesman.

James Madison (1809–17): "the father of the Constitution," having played a major role in the Constitutional Convention of 1787.

James Monroe (1817–25): promulgator of the Monroe Doctrine, which stated that "the European powers could no longer colonize or interfere with the American continents."

John Quincy Adams (1825–29): the son of John Adams. Secretary of State under Monroe, he may actually have written the Monroe Doctrine. Also an antislavery campaigner.

Abraham Lincoln (R, 1861–65): really *was* born in a log cabin. Gained national stature from his stance against slavery. His election to the presidency caused the Southern states to secede from the Union, thus beginning the Civil War. His famous Gettysburg Address—"Four score and seven years ago our fathers brought forth upon this continent a new nation, conceived in Liberty..."—further expressed his antislavery views, as did his campaign for reelection in 1864. He was shot by John Wilkes Booth five days after the surrender of the Confederate general Robert E. Lee, which effectively ended the Civil War.

Ulysses S. Grant (R, 1869–77): the leader of the Union army during the Civil War; presided over the reconstruction of the South.

James Garfield (R, 1881): assassinated by a disgruntled office-seeker after only four months in office.

William McKinley (R, 1897–1901): president during the Spanish-American War that saw the United States acquire Cuba and the Philippines. Assassinated by an anarchist in Buffalo.

Theodore Roosevelt (R, 1901–09): one of two U.S. presidents to be awarded a Nobel Peace Prize (for his role in ending the Russo-Japanese War)—the other was Woodrow Wilson. Expansionist policies included promoting the growth of the U.S. Navy and the building of the Panama Canal. A great advocate of the United States, entering the First World War.

Woodrow Wilson (D, 1913–21): avoided joining the war for several years, but in the end was forced "to make the world safe for democracy." His Fourteen-Point plan to prevent future wars formed the basis of the League of Nations (the fore-runner of the United Nations).

Warren Harding (R, 1921–23): campaigned on the issue of opposing U.S. membership of the League of Nations during Wilson's tenure; died in office under mysterious circumstances.

Calvin Coolidge (R, 1923–29): notoriously taciturn president whose economic policies were blamed for the 1929 Wall Street crash. Apparently, a woman who sat next to him at a dinner party bet him that she would get at least three words out of him in the course of the evening. "You lose" was the president's reply—and she did; he didn't say another word for the rest of the night.

Franklin D. Roosevelt (D, 1933–45): the longest-serving president in U.S. history. Stricken with polio and confined to a wheelchair throughout his presidency, he came to power at the height of the Great Depression and instituted the New Deal for economic recovery. He was president during most of World War II and died in office three weeks before Germany surrendered. His wife, Eleanor, was a noted diplomat and political adviser.

Harry S Truman (D, 1945–53): Roosevelt's vice president, who succeeded him in the last months of World War II and was responsible for the decision to drop atomic bombs on Nagasaki and Hiroshima. Also popularized the expression "The buck stops here."

Dwight D. Eisenhower (R, 1953–61): Nicknamed Ike, he was the Supreme Commander of the Allied forces during the 1944 Normandy landing. His presidency coincided with the height of the Cold War and the birth of the civil rights movement.

John F. Kennedy (D, 1961–63): the first Catholic to be elected president. He and his glamorous wife, Jackie, changed the image of the presidency. President during the Cuban Missile Crisis, which may be the nearest the world has ever come to nuclear war. Assassinated in Dallas by Lee Harvey Oswald, who was himself shot and killed by Jack Ruby two days later. The conspiracy theorists are still working on it.

Lyndon B. Johnson (D, 1963–69): Known as LBJ, he was Kennedy's vice president. The Civil Rights Act and the Voting Rights Act, which extended the voting rights of African Americans, were passed during his presidency, but Johnson is mostly remembered for his escalation of the Vietnam War and the subsequent protests.

Richard Nixon (R, 1969–74): the only U.S. president to resign under the threat of impeachment, following the scandal known as Watergate: The Democratic Party's headquarters at the Watergate Hotel had been robbed during the 1972 elections, and it became apparent that Nixon knew all about it and the subsequent cover-up. *Washington Post* journalists Bob Woodward and Carl Bernstein led the exposure—the story is told in their book *All the President's Men*, and a film based on the book was made.

Gerald Ford (R, 1974–77): the only president not to have been elected, even as vice president: Nixon appointed him after the elected vice president, Spiro Agnew, resigned over a tax scandal. Ford granted Nixon a presidential pardon for his role in Watergate.

Jimmy Carter (D, 1977–81): the peanut farmer from Georgia who brought social reform at home and was instrumental in arranging a peace treaty between Israel and Egypt. He will be most remembered for the chaos surrounding the taking of U.S. hostages in the American embassy in Iran. Carter won the Nobel Peace Prize in 2002 for his international peacekeeping efforts, work in human rights, and economic development.

Ronald Reagan (R, 1981–89): former Hollywood film star and long-term governor of California before becoming president. Introduced the anti-Russian Strategic Defense Initiative (known as Star Wars) but later reached an arms-reduction agreement with the USSR. Reagan ordered military action in Granada, an island north of Venezuela. His administration is also remembered for the Iran-Contra affair. In 1981 there was an unsuccessful assassination attempt against him that provoked his remark, "Honey, I forgot to duck."

George H. W. Bush (R, 1989–93): a former West Texas oil executive before becoming president, his political posts included director of the Central Intelligence Agency and vice president in Ronald Reagan's administration. He took the world into the first Gulf War and ordered military action in Panama, and was in office when the Berlin Wall fell and the Soviet Union collapsed. His popularity at home declined when he broke a campaign promise to lower taxes. Bush is the father of the forty-third president George W. Bush and Jeb Bush, former governor of Florida.

Bill Clinton (D, 1993–2001): young, charismatic, Clinton spent a lot of time in the headlines because of his alleged affair with a White House intern. Married to Hillary, who ran, unsuccessfully, for the 2008 democratic presidential nomination.

George W. Bush (R, 2001–2009): a former partner of the Texas Rangers baseball team and governor of Texas, Bush was elected president in 2000, receiving a majority of the electoral votes, but narrowly losing the popular vote. In his first term he enacted "No Child Left Behind," a measure later signed into law that aimed to close the gap between rich and poor student performance. After the September 11, 2001 attacks on the United States, he initiated a global war on terrorism and launched attacks on Afghanistan and Iraq.

Canadian Prime Ministers

Prime Minister Pierre Trudeau once said: "Living next to the Americans is like sleeping next to an elephant—no matter how friendly and even-tempered the elephant, one is affected by every twitch!" It takes a certain kind of character to cope with such sleeping arrangements, as well as the challenges that come with running the second largest (in area) country in the world. Here are the top politicians that Canadians voted in and out.

Sir John A. Macdonald (1867–73; 1878–91): a Scottish-born lawyer with a soft spot for hard drink, he shepherded the country from being a rump of four tiny provinces into a vast nation linked from sea to sea by a brand-new transcontinental railway. A champion of Canadian autonomy within the British Empire as well as the status of the French in public institutions, the Conservative PM is also remembered for the binge drinking that dogged him during his time in office.

Alexander Mackenzie (1873–78): emigrated from his native Scotland at age 20 in pursuit of the girl he loved. As the country's first Liberal head of government, Mackenzie established the Supreme Court and founded the Royal Military College. A staunch democrat proud of his working-class roots, the former stonemason turned down an offer of knighthood three times.

Sir John Abbott (1891–92) son of an Anglican priest and two-term mayor of Montreal. The Conservative also happened to be the great-grandfather of Hollywood actor Christopher Plummer.

John Thompson (1892–94): Conservative PM who suffered a stroke and promptly died during a visit to Windsor Castle. Queen Victoria was not amused.

Mackenzie Bowell (1894-96): forced to resign by his own cabinet ministers, this prominent Orangeman lived long and prospered, dying in his 95th year.

Sir Charles Tupper (1896): Conservative who served the shortest period in office of any prime minister: 69 days. On the other hand, his marriage to wife Frances Morse lasted the longest: 66 years.

Sir Wilfrid Laurier (1896–1911): once decreed: "The nineteenth century was the century of the United States. I think we can claim that Canada will fill the twentieth century." During the Liberal's 15 years as head of government, Laurier witnessed an era of unprecedented immigration, infrastructure expansion, and the creation of two new western provinces.

Robert Borden (1911–20): last prime minister to be born before Confederation, whose bold commitment to the war effort precipitated the Conscription Crisis. This cost the Conservative the support of many French-speaking Canadians. His face adorns the Canadian $100 bill.

Arthur Meighen (1920–21; 1926): the Ontario-born prime minister. The son of a farmer, he studied mathematics and physics at the University of Toronto. The Conservative was instrumental in creating the Canadian National Railways system.

Mackenzie King (1921–26; 1926–30; 1935–48): grandson of William Lyon Mackenzie, leader of the 1837 Rebellion in Upper Canada. As Canada's longest-serving prime minister, this Liberal led the country for 22 years. King was a bachelor who had a penchant for holding séances and talking to his dog. But he was also a capable politician and statesman. He steered the country through much of the Depression as well as World War II. A social reformer, his government brought in unemployment insurance and family allowances.

Richard Bennett (1930–35): elected on the eve of the Great Depression, he was Canada's only prime minister to be buried abroad. It took the Conservative several years to implement radical economic reforms, but by then it was too late for his government. After his defeat he moved to England, where he died.

Louis St. Laurent (1948–57): dubbed Uncle Louis for his folksy and avuncular campaigning style, he staked Canada's global role as an important middle power. His Liberal administration got the ball rolling on the Trans-Canada Highway and St. Lawrence Seaway, welcomed Newfoundland into Confederation, and oversaw Canadian participation in the Korean War.

John Diefenbaker (1957–63): set out to make Canadian citizenship more inclusive to people of diverse origins, with an emphasis on aboriginal peoples. The Progressive Conservative appointed the first female federal cabinet minister, Ellen Fairclough, and was an outspoken opponent of apartheid in South Africa. But economic and fiscal woes, as well as his decision to scrap the Avro Arrow jet project, led to his government's demise.

Lester Pearson (1963–68): considered to be the "inventor" of U.N. peacekeeping, for which he won the 1957 Nobel Peace Prize, his Liberal government initiated federal bilingualism, established a national pension plan, signed the Auto Pact with the United States, introduced universal Medicare, and unveiled a new national flag. A well-rounded athlete, Pearson played semipro baseball in Ontario and hockey while studying at Oxford.

Pierre Elliott Trudeau (1968–79; 1980–84): not only a swinging playboy, but also a no-nonsense gunslinger. When rioters hurled objects at him during a 1968 ceremony, he refused to withdraw to safety. When separatist terrorists took hostages in Quebec, he sent in the army. He stuck it to the Alberta oil barons during the energy crisis of the 1970s. He made mincemeat of his main opponent during the 1980 referendum on Quebec sovereignty. A Liberal, he brought in official bilingualism, the metric system, and—in his proudest moment—repatriated the Constitution, to which he added the Charter of Rights and Freedoms. Fidel Castro, his good friend, was among the pallbearers at his funeral.

Joe Clark (1979–80): dismissed as "Joe Who?" during his early years on the national stage, this Progressive Conservative politician astounded the pundits when he was elected Canada's youngest-ever prime minister at age 39.

John Turner (1984): dashing, dapper, and athletic, he inherited the prime minister's job after Pierre Trudeau retired. The Liberal is remembered for his tooth-and-nails crusade against the proposed free-trade deal with the United States.

Brian Mulroney (1984–93): won the largest majority government in Canadian history in 1994. The Progressive Conservative soon came under fire for his cozy friendship with U.S. president Bush, a revolving door of scandals, and ill-advised tinkering with the Constitution. Nevertheless, his administration hammered out the 1988 Free Trade Agreement with the United States and the 1992 North American Free Trade Agreement.

Kim Campbell (1993): Canada's first female prime minister, who voters never actually gave a mandate to rule. Instead, she briefly inherited the reigns of power, only to go down to a prompt and decisive defeat.

Jean Chrétien (1993–2003): eighteenth child of a paper-mill worker, he was a seasoned veteran of Liberal cabinets dating back to the 1960s. A brilliant, if rustic, campaigner, his long experience and political instincts won him three consecutive majority governments.

Paul Martin (2003–6): as a Liberal three-time finance minister, he has been credited with getting Canada's fiscal health into shape. The scion of a wealthy shipping family, he faced the electorate, but once as prime minister won a short-lived minority mandate.

Stephen Harper (2006–present): the current prime minister, he represents a Conservative party that removed the word Progressive from its official name. An influential back-room player whose survival skills brought him to the fore, Harper has consolidated power in the prime minister's office as rarely seen before.

Notable Kings and Queens of England

House	Name	Known for
Normandy	William I (1066–87)	Won Battle of Hastings, created the feudal system.
Plantagenet	Henry II (1154–89)	Son of Matilda, the one who conflicted with Thomas à Becket.
	Richard I (1189–99)	The Lionheart, fought the Crusades. Depicted as good king in Robin Hood stories.
	John (1199–1216)	Richard's brother, the wicked Prince John in Robin Hood. Forced to sign Magna Carta.
	Edward I (1272–1307)	Conquered most of Wales, built many castles, son was titled Prince of Wales. Died fighting the Scottish.
Lancaster	Henry IV (1399–1413)	Richard's cousin Henry Bolingbroke. Battled Welsh prince Owen Glendower and Henry Percy of Northumberland.
	Henry V (1413–22)	Shakespeare's Prince Hal, has merry dealings with Falstaff but grows up to win the battle of Agincourt.
York	Edward IV (1461–83, briefly deposed 1470–71)	Great-great grandson of Edward III; brought back with help of cousin Richard Neville, who later betrayed him.
	Richard III (1483-85)	Uncle of Ed V; depicted by Shakespeare and others as wicked hunchback/mass murderer. Defeated at battle of Bosworth.
Tudor	Henry VII (1485–1509)	Defeated Richard III, taking the throne more by force than by lineage, effectively ending the War of the Roses.
	Henry VIII (1509–47)	Six wives: Catherine, Anne, Jane, Anne, Catherine, Catherine; often remembered as divorced, beheaded, died, divorced, beheaded, survived.

House	Name	Known for
Tudor (continued)	Mary I (1553–58)	Older sister of Edward VI, daughter of Catherine of Aragon. Overthrew Lady Jane Grey and had her beheaded.
	Elizabeth I (1558–1603)	Mary's sister, daughter of Anne Boleyn. Defeated the Spanish Armada. Beheaded Mary Queen of Scots, but since Liz had no heir, Mary's son became king.
Stuart	James I (1603–25)	Already James VI of Scotland, Mary's son. Oversaw the translation of the Bible.
	Charles I (1625–49)	Believed in the Divine Right of Kings. Did whatever he wanted and was beheaded as a result.
Stuarts, Restored	Charles II (1660–85)	The Merry Monarch, reintroduced theater. Ruled during the Great Plague and the Great Fire of London.
	Anne (1702–14)	First sovereign under a unified England and Scotland. Died without living children. Throne went to the Hanoverians.
Hanover	George I (1714–27)	Never really mastered English, lived in Hanover most of his life.
	George III (1760–1820)	The mad one who lost the American colonies after the Revolutionary War.
Saxe–Coburg–Gotha	Victoria (1837–1901)	Longest-reigning monarch. Her children married diplomatically; most royal houses of Europe are, in some way, descended from her.
Windsor	George V (1910–36)	King during WWI, the General Strike and Great Depression. Valuable political advisor.
	George VI (1936–52)	Brother of edward VIII. Ruled during WWII, wife Elizabeth known as Queen Mother.
	Elizabeth II (1952–)	The present queen. Mother of Prince Charles; former mother-in-law to Lady Di.

Major World Conflicts

Times may change, but the issues that incite wars among people around the world remain the same: Power, territory, religion, and resources are usually at the heart of the matter.

☞ 1066: BATTLE OF HASTINGS

The year 1066 was a busy one. King Edward the Confessor died on January 5, leaving four claimants to the throne. The legitimate heir, Edward's son Edgar, was a child and no one took much notice of him. Military expediency preferred the successful Saxon general Harold Godwin, but there was also the Norwegian king, Harald Hardrada, who invaded northern England and, on September 25, was defeated by Harold at Stamford Bridge, near York. Three days later an army led by William of Normandy (to whom Harold Godwin may or may not have promised allegiance in a visit to Normandy the previous year) landed at Pevensey in Sussex, some 249 miles (400 km) away. Harold marched to meet him, and the battle now known as Hastings took place on October 14. Harold was killed (tradition has it by an arrow in his eye), and on Christmas Day, William the Conqueror was crowned King William I.

☞ 1337–1453: HUNDRED YEARS WAR

A war between England and France. Primarily a dispute over territory because parts of France, notably the prosperous wine-growing areas of Gascony and Aquitaine, had come into English possession through a succession of strategic marriages. The battles include: Crécy (1346), at which Edward III's son, the Black Prince, "won his spurs;" Poitiers (1356), when the French king, John II, was captured and held for ransom; and Harfleur and Agincourt (both 1415), when English archers won the day. After Henry V's early death in 1422, a French resurgence inspired by Joan of Arc gradually pushed the English back, until in 1453 the French won a decisive victory at Castillon and reclaimed all of the southwest part of the country. Only Calais remained in English possession.

☞ 1455–85: WARS OF THE ROSES

A series of civil wars between the English royal houses of York and Lancaster. In a nutshell, Edward III had far too many descendants who thought they ought to be in charge. Key battles were, Wakefield (1460), in which Richard, Duke of York, leader of the opposition to the Lancastrian Henry VI, was killed; and Tewkesbury (1471), a Yorkist victory, shortly after which Henry VI died—probably murdered—in the Tower of London. Rivalry between the in-laws of the new (Yorkist) king, Edward IV, the numerous and opportunistic Woodvilles, and other members of the aristocracy ensured that conflict continued. It culminated in the Battle of Bosworth (1485), when Henry Tudor, a Lancastrian descended from an illegitimate son of Edward III's son, John of Gaunt, defeated and killed the Yorkist Richard III and became Henry VII.

☞ 1622-1917: THE AMERICAN INDIAN WARS

In the past, American history books have conveniently skimmed over or skipped the Indian wars altogether. A few early proprietors, such as William Penn, formed alliances with the Native American people, even learning to speak their language, but a large number of the early settlers encroached upon Indian territory, defied treaties, monopolized game, and practiced outright slaughter of the Native Americans. In some cases the Native Americans attacked first, but most often they felt threatened. The Pequot War of 1637, one of the earliest skirmishes, essentially eliminated the power of the Pequot tribe in present-day New England; most were killed, others were sold into slavery. The Indian wars were eventually fought in other parts of the East, the Great Plains, the Southwest, and in California. Some of the wars include Tecumseh (the Creek War), the Texas-Indian Wars, the Battle of Little Big Horn (Custer's Last Stand), the Wounded Knee Massacre, the Navajo and Apache conflicts, the California Indian wars, and many more. Native Americans were killed, relocated, or escaped to Canada. The 10th Cavalry Regiment, an African-American unit that the Native Americans termed Buffalo Soldiers, fought one of the last battles in 1917.

☞ **1759: THE BATTLE OF THE PLAINS OF ABRAHAM**
A significant turning point in North American history, the British rout over French forces at the Battle of the Plains of Abraham near Quebec City on September 13 was an important milestone for the ascendant British Empire. This battle by land and sea that cost the lives of the commanding generals on both sides all but eradicated France's colonial role in the New World. It also helped set the stage for the American War of Independence less than two decades later.

☞ 1775–83: AMERICAN WAR OF INDEPENDENCE, OR THE REVOLUTIONARY WAR

The clue is in the title, really. The thirteen British colonies in North America revolted against British rule, specifically against taxation without representation. The Boston Tea Party (1773) was an act of direct action, which helped spark the American Revolution. Late on the night of April 18, 1775, a silversmith named Paul Revere recieved word that the British posed an imminent threat, which Longfellow preserved in the infamous poem *Paul Revere's Ride* ("Listen my children and you shall hear..."). Early battles at Lexington and Concord (the shot heard 'round the world) were followed by the Battle of Bunker Hill, which was really fought on Breed's Hill. The Declaration of Independence was signed in 1776, and battles followed across what are now the northeastern United States and eastern Canada. George Washington, the American commander-in-chief, led troops across the Delaware River to mount an attack upon the British and Hessian troops. This success at the Battle of Trenton (1776) marked the turning point of the war. France, Spain, and Holland all sided with the Americans—the Dutch gained control of the English Channel and threatened to invade Britain. Britain finally acknowledged American independence by the Treaty of Paris (1783).

☞ 1789: FRENCH REVOLUTION

The French finally had enough of the Bourbon kings and overthrew them, storming the state prison, the Bastille, on July 14, mobbing the palace of Versailles and eventually beheading King Louis XVI and his queen, Marie Antoinette. The revolutionaries proclaimed a republic, but the moderate

Girondins were ousted by the more extreme Jacobins. Power passed to the hands of the Committee of Public Safety (one of those names that you can just tell is going to lead to trouble). Georges Danton, initially one of the most important members of the committee, was superceded by a lawyer named Maximilien Robespierre, and the ensuing Reign of Terror saw the execution of thousands of alleged antirevolutionaries. Perhaps inevitably, Danton and Robespierre both also ended up on the guillotine.

☞ 1792–1815: NAPOLEONIC WARS

Napoleon Bonaparte rose to prominence in the aftermath of the French Revolution, and was in charge of the French army fighting the Austrians in Italy by 1796. Next he decided to break down the British Empire by conquering Egypt. Defeated by the British admiral Horatio Nelson at the Battle of the Nile (1799), he returned to France, overthrew the Executive Directory (the post-revolutionary government), became consul and then emperor in 1804—and he was 35 years old. The following year, he was again defeated by Nelson (at Trafalgar, where Nelson was killed) but did better on land, winning victories at Austerlitz, Jena–Averstedt, and Friedland and more or less conquering continental Europe. The British Duke of Wellington, Arthur Wellesley, defeated him in the Iberian Peninsula—a subsection of the Napoleonic wars known as the Peninsular War (1808–14), in the course of which Napoleon also found time to march on Moscow, losing about 400,000 of his 500,000-strong army in the harsh Russian winter. He was defeated again at Leipzig in 1813, forced to abdicate, and exiled to Elba, an island off the coast of Italy. He escaped, resumed power for the

"Hundred Days," and was finally defeated in 1815 at the battle of Waterloo, and exiled again, this time to the remote South Atlantic island of St. Helena, where he died in 1821.

☞ 1812–15: THE WAR OF 1812

Contrary to its name, this war lasted almost three years. The British were invading American ships and putting its sailors into servitude. And a British sea blockade on France during the Napoleonic Wars made trade difficult (although New England opposed the war and was trading with Britain and Canada). The British also didn't appreciate that forces within the United States were moving into the Northwest Territories and the Canadian border. However, British and Mohawk forces stood ready for a U.S. advance and many American soldiers were taken prisoner at the Battle of Beaver Dams. This war ended with the conclusion of the Napoleonic War when the British fleet pulled out of its blockade, and the Treaty of Ghent took effect in 1815. Since, technically, the United States was not defeated (although it took a beating), the war was considered a stalemate, with both sides going back to their corners and calling it a day. The United States considered the war a confirmation of its independence because they stuck together, once again, and fought bravely.

☞ 1846–48: THE MEXICAN-AMERICAN WAR

The bankrupt Mexican government had a loose hold on Texas and its northern and western provinces (the West) after it won its own independence from Spain. American settlers in the Texas region, such as a group led by Colonel Davy Crockett, fought a war of independence from Mexican forces in the area (remember the Alamo?). With many losses the Texas settlers eventually won this war and proclaimed annexation from Mexico in 1845, but Mexico did not recognize this secession. The Texans and Western states obtained support from the U.S. government. Although many Whigs in the United States opposed the war, many southern Democrats, who wished to gain territory and expand slavery, held the belief of Manifest Destiny, proclaiming that the United States was somehow divinely destined to expand from the Atlantic seaboard to the Pacific Ocean. Mexico and the United States disagreed regarding borders, and after more skirmishes and battles the United States declared war on Mexico in May 1846. Author Henry David Thoreau refused to pay his taxes as a protest to the war and was put in jail for a night as a result—an incident that inspired him to write an essay that was later dubbed "Civil Disobedience," which stated that individuals should not allow the government to sway or overrule their own sense of conscience, especially in true matters of injustice. Ultimately, the United States won the war and signed the Treaty of Guadalupe Hidalgo, which required Mexico to secede not only Texas but also parts of Colorado, Arizona, New Mexico, and Wyoming as well as all of California, Nevada, and Utah in return for $15 million.

☞ 1861–65: AMERICAN CIVIL WAR

Eleven breakaway Confederate states objected to the antislavery sentiments of the North. These sentiments (and eventual policies) had their roots in the Abolitionist Movement, which was spearheaded by Northern Transcendentalists such as

Ralph Waldo Emerson, Henry David Thoreau, and Louisa May Alcott, and in large part by Harriet Beecher Stowe's novel, *Uncle Tom's Cabin*.

The Southern plantations had become well off from the extremely profitable combination of slavery and the Cotton Gin (Eli Whitney's then recent invention). This fact, combined with Southern fears regarding the North's control of the banking system, would lead to the idea of states' rights, from which was born the Confederacy of the Southern states.

Eventually a geographic border divided the North from South and became known as the Mason-Dixon Line. The Confederate secession was led by Jefferson Davis, and the war began with a Confederate attack on Fort Sumter, South Carolina (the first state to secede from the Union). Later key encounters included the Confederate victory at Bull Run, Confederate General Stonewall Jackson's campaign in Shenandoah, and the Union victories in the Seven Days' Battle and at Gettysburg (where Lincoln delivered the famous Gettysburg Address).

The Battle of Gettysburg lasted for three days and is still considered the largest battle in the history of the Western Hemisphere. The casualties of the war were horrific, with as many as 23,000 dead and wounded at the Battle of Antietam alone, which to this day remains the single bloodiest day in American history. After this battle, President Lincoln announced the Emancipation Proclamation, which freed "all people." After Union general William T. Sherman's brutal march through the South in 1864 and the capture of Atlanta and Savannah, much of the South would soon be in Union control. Within months Confederate general Robert E. Lee (who commanded the feared army of Northern Virginia), would surrender to future president Ulysses S. Grant at Appomattox Court House. Following the Union victory and the assassination of Abraham Lincoln, there was a painful reconstruction period in the South, where some cities, such as Vicksburg, would not celebrate the Fourth of July until 1938.

☞ 1880–81 and 1899–1902: BOER WARS

These were revolutionary wars fought by the Afrikaners (Boers, descended from Dutch settlers) of South Africa against British rule. The first, in which the Boers were led by Paul Kruger, gained a degree of independence for Transvaal, which became known as the South African Republic. The second involved lengthy Boer sieges of Ladysmith and Mafeking. Lord Horatio Kitchener was one of the leaders of the British forces; Robert Baden-Powell, who went on to found the Boy Scouts, distinguished himself in the siege of Mafeking. British public and political opinion was polarized by the second Boer War, and it led to a lot of rising and falling of governments.

☞ 1914–18: WORLD WAR I

The principal players were an alliance of Britain, France, Russia, and others (the Allied Powers, united by the Entente Cordiale and later the Triple Entente), against Germany, Austro-Hungary, and Turkey (the Central Powers); the United States joined in 1917. The complicated causes included the Allies' fear of German expansion in Europe and various colonies, particularly in Africa; and a conflict of interest between Russia and Austro-Hungary in the Balkans.

Although war was looming for years, it was sparked by the assassination of the Archduke Franz Ferdinand, heir to the Austro-Hungarian throne, by a Serb nationalist, Gabriel Princip. Austro-Hungary declared war on Serbia, Russia backed the Serbs, and you can guess the rest. Much of "The Great War" took place on what is known as the Western Front in the trenches of northeastern France and Belgium after Germany's thwarted attempt to invade France and take over Paris. It is most notable for the horrific loss of life: over a million men in the Battle of the Somme alone, with Ypres and Passchendaele not much better. On the Eastern Front the Gallipoli Campaign in Turkey killed many Australians and New Zealanders. The Central powers not only suffered great loss of life but were losing resources and support on the homefront, which led them to agree to the armistice treaty and subsequently the Treaty of Versailles, which ended the fighting.

Some of the provisions of the treaty required Germany and its allies take full responsibility for the war, pay reparations, and essentially redraw the map of Europe. Austria-Hungary was sliced into Austria, Hungary, Czechoslavakia, and Yugoslavia. The Ottoman Empire was distributed among the Allied Powers (with the Turkish core remaining as the Republic of Turkey). The western frontier of the Russian Empire became Estonia, Finland, Latvia, Lithuania, and Poland. As a result of the treaty, the League of Nations (later replaced by the United Nations) was founded to help countries settle disputes through negotiation, diplomacy, and the global improvement of the quality of life.

☞ 1917: RUSSIAN REVOLUTION

Actually two revolutions—one in February and one in October of the same year. The first, sparked by a shortage of food, led to the abdication of the Romanov czar Nicholas II; the second involved the Bolsheviks (led by Vladimir Lenin and Trotsky) seizing power, executing most of the royal family, and establishing the first communist state. A civil war between the "Red" Bolsheviks and the anticommunist "White" Russians lasted until 1921. After Lenin died in 1924, Trotsky lost a power struggle with Stalin, went into exile in Mexico, and was murdered there.

☞ 1939–45: WORLD WAR II

Hitler rose to power in Germany in the early 1930s and proceeded to take over various parts of Europe. Britain and France had promised to protect Polish neutrality, so they were forced to declare war when Germany invaded Poland. The Berlin, Rome, Tokyo pact bound Germany, Italy, and Japan together, known as the Axis powers.

Hitler's invasion of France led to the evacuation of hundreds of thousands of Allied forces, many of them in small boats, from Dunkirk, in 1940; Britain now faced the threat of invasion and months of bombing (the Blitz). The war in the air that followed (1940–41) is known as the Battle of Britain. The previously neutral United States began selling arms and goods to Great Britain, provided it sent its own ships to U.S. ports for "cash and carry."

In 1940 the United States implemented a series of embargoes against Japan, and in September of that same year, the United

States agreed to swap American destroyers for British bases. In December 1941 the Japanese bombed the Hawaiian naval base at Pearl Harbor, bringing the United States into the war and opening up a whole new theater of conflict in the Pacific.

Exactly six months after Pearl Harbor, the U.S. Navy defeated a Japanese attack of the Midway Islands, sinking four Japanese carriers and a warship. This defense severely weakened Japanese Naval power, turning the tide in the United State's favor. The Battle of the Japanese island, Iwo Jima, constituted another hard-fought victory for the Allied forces and was a stepping-stone toward the Japanese heartland. The Japanese had built an elaborate bunker and tunnel system on the island through Mount Suribachi. Allied forces used flamethrowers and grenades to clear them out. Eventually the Japanese ran out of water, food, and supplies. Most of the 21,000 Japanese soldiers fought to their deaths, and one in four U.S. soldiers died during the attack—over 26,500. One of the most reproduced photographs in history is the flag raising by U.S. soldiers on the top of the mountain, which was converted into a statue at Arlington Cemetery and a war memorial in Harlingen, Texas. Three of the six flag raisers would die soon after the photograph was taken.

After Iwo Jima, another major win for the Allied forces—the Battle of Okinawa—took more lives than the atomic bombs later dropped on Hiroshima and Nagasaki. Kamikazes, or suicide aviation bombers, sunk almost 34 Allied ships and crafts of all kind, damaging 368; the fleet lost 763 aircraft. The cost of this battle in lives, time, and material weighed heavily on the decision to drop the atomic bombs six weeks later, which forced the Japanese to surrender.

Far away, Germany made the mistake of attacking western Russia in July of 1942. The Russians held out in Stalingrad and launched a counteroffensive in the bloodiest battle in human history, with combined casualties of over 1.5 million. The Nazis were held up in the winter on their way to Moscow, some freezing to death. The Germans were ill-equipped and ill-prepared for winter conflict. Stalingrad continued until February 1943, when the last German forces surrendered. This paved the way for the Normandy (D-Day) landings in June 1944, the turning point for Germany, which surrendered in May 1945.

The Holocaust. Prior to and during the war, the German country became involved in state-supported genocide of Jewish people (the Holocaust or Shoah). Many German nationalists held deep-seated resentment, hatred, and prejudice against the Jewish people. Before World War II the Depression hit Germany hard, especially because of reparations required after World War I. Germans blamed communists for WW I, calling it a Judeo-Bolshevist conspiracy and even went so far as to blame Jewish Bankers for the Treaty of Versailles. Many Germans resented Jewish successes and felt that the Jewish people were taking German jobs. Hitler believed in supremacy of the German/Aryan race and considered Jewish, Polish, gay, Gypsies, Slavs, Russian, and mentally challenged people as subhuman. Hitler preached hatred, and the ignorant masses followed, looking for a scapegoat for their desperate situation. Some believed the propaganda that the Jews were being jailed for their "crimes," whereas others simply went along in fear of the Nazis as they essentially brutally beat up or killed anyone who opposed their power.

☞ 1950–53: THE KOREAN WAR

After WWII Korea was divided into the communist Northern half and the American-occupied South, with the dividing line at the 38th parallel. This war began when the North Korean communist army, armed with Soviet tanks, invaded South Korea. Although the territory was not strategically important to the United States, a deep-seated fear of communism led to the country's involvement in what was termed a police action, so Congress did not need to make an official declaration of war. General Douglas MacArthur and his U.S. and U.N. troops orchestrated an invasion of Inchon and then recaptured Seoul, passing the 38th parallel to the Northern side, which prompted China to send in troops to protect its interests in Manchuria. MacArthur continued to push northward until he was relieved of his duties by President Truman, a politically unpopular move since MacArthur was a WWII war hero. Both sides tried to negotiate a peace treaty but disagreed over many of the provisions, so fighting continued. In 1953 at Panmunjom, a treaty was signed that brought about a cease-fire and returned the divided line to its prewar coordinates. The war would later inspire the novel and subsequent film and television series *M*A*S*H*, about the doctors and support staff stationed at the 4077th Mobile Army Surgical Hospital, which was located near Ouijongbu during the war.

☞ THE COLD WAR

Difficult to date because it wasn't really a war, but a period of intense mutual distrust between former World War II Allies— the United States, U.K., and France on the one hand and the

USSR on the other—at its height during the 1950s. Winston Churchill coined the term "iron curtain" for the ideological and political barrier that separated east from west. Tensions began to diminish during the 1970s and 1980s, especially with the introduction by Mikhail Gorbachev of the policies of *glasnost* (openness) and *perestroika* (reconstruction—specifically of the economy), which led to the breakup of the USSR.

☞ 1959–75: THE VIETNAM WAR

Much of the fighting occurred between 1964 and 1975 in South Vietnam and bordering areas of Cambodia and Laos. Several bombing runs over North Vietnam also occurred.

The United States, Australia, New Zealand, and South Korea all joined forces with the Republic of Vietnam to fight the North, with its communist-led South Vietnamese guerrilla movement and the National Liberation Front backed by USSR-supplied weaponry.

The seeds of the Vietnam War were planted during the First Indochinese War, when the communists, under Ho Chi Minh, fought the French for independence. After a socialist state was established in the North, mass killings of "class enemies" followed. Eventually, a U.S.-backed government in the South launched its own anticommunist campaign. However, the South's autocratic and nepotistic president, Ngo Dinh Diem, had trouble with insurgencies. The CIA apparently alerted generals in the South that the United States would support a coup, and Diem was eventually assassinated. This caused chaos in the South, and the Viet Cong gained ground.

At this point U.S. president John F. Kennedy increased U.S. forces in the area to help train troops. Three weeks after Diem's death, Kennedy was also assassinated. The Vietnamese War was fraught with controversy; some Americans strongly feared a communist scourge, whereas others did not feel that the United States should police the world, toppling regimes out of fear, causing even more unrest. President Nixon ordered a suspension of the action in 1973 and soon afterward signed the Paris Peace Accords, which ended U.S. involvement in the conflict. After that, the North ignored the cease-fire agreement, invaded the South, taking Saigon (being renamed Ho Chi Minh City), and forming the Socialist Republic of Vietnam. Many supporters of the South were jailed or executed.

☞ 1991: THE GULF WAR

The Gulf War involved the high-tech conflict between Kuwait and U.N.-led forces against Iraq in order to remove Iraq forces that overran Kuwait in a surprise assault. The Iraqis claimed that the Kuwaitis were stealing their oil through slant drilling on the border. This war was largely fought from the air and from tanks, with U.N. forces grossly outnumbering the Iraqi forces. U.N. forces liberated Kuwait and attacked southern Iraq. The troops pulled out after Iraq agreed to a U.N. resolution requiring the Middle Eastern country to destroy major weapons, not develop new ones, and cease its support of terrorists groups.

☞ 2003–PRESENT: THE IRAQ WAR

The U.S. sought to remove the corrupt Iraqi government and military establishment from power. The American government claimed that the Iraqis were hiding weapons of mass destruction. And it also hoped to protect and secure U.S. interests in the Middle East, which many people believe to be oil. Many U.N. allies opposed the war, especially the Arab countries, but an abbreviated coalition was sent into Iraq nonetheless, toppling the Saddam Hussein regime. Through the years, a long and continued war in Iraq has lost popularity with most U.S. citizens, but the plan to exit the country was not as well executed as the plan to enter, and many fear the inevitable civil unrest that may ensue upon U.S. departure. Others fear that pouring manpower and trillions of dollars into a war that could last for many years could have futile and catastrophic consequences to a nation that needs to concentrate its money and human resources into conservation and clean and renewable energy.

African American History

Another scantly covered period in American history involves the mass atrocities committed against Africans; they were kidnapped, captured, and sold into slavery. Revolts ensued but were quashed. African Americans persisted and held strong against their persecutors, eventually gaining freedom after the Civil War and affecting major positive changes in the United States and Canada. This small section cannot do justice to the major obstacles that were overcome and the progressive advances made by the African American community. Slavery was finally abolished in 1865 by the 13th Amendment of the

Constitution, and less than 150 years later Barack Obama, of
half-Kenyan ancestry, announced his candidacy for president
of the United States.

☞ SLAVERY

In 1619 a Dutch trader exchanged Africans for food in
the marketplace of Jamestown, Virginia. By the 1660s a
race-based slave system became popular with tobacco
planters in the American South, who at the time also enslaved
Native Americans; slavery soon spread among the colonies.
Slaves were not treated as people but as property; they were
mistreated, punished harshly, and killed. In the 1700s
England's abolitionists, and later the Quakers, within the
colonies sought to petition government against slavery. The
American abolitionist movement began to gain ground. In
1793 Eli Whitney patented his invention, the cotton gin,
increasing demand and production of U.S.-grown cotton.
Although this proved positive for the economy, it caused a
resurge in slavery trade, especially in the cotton-growing
South, since farmers needed more workers to glean the cotton.
In the North small progress was being made, and in 1830 the
first National Negro Convention was held in Philadelphia,
where one point of discussion involved emigration to Canada.

☞ THE UNDERGROUND RAILROAD

The date marking the start of this movement remains
unknown. During the 19th century Canada played a key role in
the battle to abolish slavery, with at least 30,000 slaves escaping
by secret routes to flee enslavement in the American South.

This political movement crossed the racial and geographic borders and exemplified Thoreau's concept of civil disobedience, which also planted the seeds for the women's suffrage movement. In 1790, Philadelphia became Underground-Railroad Central for the Northern states, since it contained a large number of emancipated black individuals and Quakers. In fact, Harriet Tubman originally escaped to Philadelphia before conducting 13 missions for the Underground Railroad to free slaves; she would later serve as a Union spy in the Civil War, and then struggled for the women's suffrage.

As a youngster, a man named John Brown traveled northeastern Ohio guiding fugitives and vowed to dedicate his life to the freedom of slaves. In 1847 he laid out his plans to raid slave plantations and route the freed people through the Appalachian Mountains to a safe haven near Lake Placid, New York. Brown would free slaves by any means necessary. He met violence with more violence, meeting his own brutal fate during an unsuccessful raid at Harper's Ferry in 1859.

A year later the Southern States seceded from the Union, followed by the American Civil War, where emancipated blacks fought bravely in the Union Army for their own freedom.

Other Important Historical Dates

This small section just didn't fit anywhere else, but most of us will remember at least something about these notable events:

☞ **1215: MAGNA CARTA, OR THE GREAT CHARTER**
Signed by King John at Runnymede, this was the first successful attempt to control the power of the English monarchy.

☞ 1453: FALL OF CONSTANTINOPLE

You might not think it was a big deal (after all, cities were falling all over the place all of the time), but this was when the Muslim Ottoman Empire took over the Byzantine, or Christian, capital of the Eastern Roman Empire, and all those scholarly monks fled into Western Europe, taking their books with them. In other words, it marked the start of the Renaissance—which, in its narrowest sense, means a rebirth in interest in classic literature, art, and architecture.

☞ 1605: GUNPOWDER PLOT

A failed attempt by a group of provincial English Catholics to blow up the Protestant king, James I, and the Houses of Parliament. Somebody let it be known, and Guy Fawkes was caught in the cellars under the Palace of Westminster with a load of gunpowder.

☞ 1620: PILGRIM FATHERS

A group of Puritans, persecuted in England because of their religion, set sail from Southampton in the *Mayflower* and in due course established a colony in Plymouth, Massachusetts.

☞ EARLY 18TH CENTURY ONWARD: AGRICULTURAL REVOLUTION

Larger, enclosed fields, inventions such as Jethro Tull's planting drill, and the concept of crop rotation pioneered by Viscount "Turnip" Townshend improved agricultural methods and increased food yield, which made it possible to feed the increasing numbers of people not working on the land following the Industrial Revolution.

~~~~~~

☞ 1750 ONWARD: INDUSTRIAL REVOLUTION

The invention of Arkwright's water-powered spinning frame, Hargreaves's spinning jenny, and Crompton's mule revolutionized the production of yarn and therefore cloth, leading to the development of factories and mass production.

Explorers

Since this chapter has been talking about fighting over many regions of the world, here is a quick rundown of people who discovered some of them.

Eric the Red and **Leif Eriksson** (late 10th–11th century, Norwegian): father and son. Eric, brought up in Iceland, was the first European to settle in Greenland; Leif, blown (a long way) off course on his way from Iceland to Greenland, became the first European to reach America. He landed at a place he called Vinland, which may have been modern-day Newfoundland or Nova Scotia.

Bartolomeu Dias (*c.* 1450–*c.* 1500, Portuguese): trade routes to India were the big thing after the Turks blocked off the land route. Dias made an attempt at doing it by sea, being the first to round the Cape of Good Hope at the bottom of Africa. But he named it the Cape of Storms, which may suggest why his crew made him turn back before they got farther than Mozambique.

Christopher Columbus (1451–1506, Italian): born in Genoa but had his voyages sponsored by Ferdinand and Isabella of Spain. The idea was to reach the East (that is, Asia) by sailing west, thus proving beyond all doubt that the Earth was round. Of course, America got in the way. Columbus never actually reached mainland North America, but he did discover the Bahamas, Hispaniola, Guadeloupe, Jamaica, and Puerto Rico, among others. His ships were the *Niña,* the *Pinta,* and the *Santa Maria.*

Amerigo Vespucci (1454–1512, Italian): discovered the mouth of the Amazon and the River Plate, which made him important enough to have a continent or two named after him.

Vasco da Gama (*c.* 1469–1525, Portuguese): persisted where Dias had failed and made it to Calicut in India.

Francisco Pizarro (*c.* 1478–1541, Spanish): the conqueror (or *conquistador*) of Peru and destroyer of the Incan Empire.

Ferdinand Magellan (*c.* 1480–1521, Portuguese): leader of the first expedition to sail around the world, although he was murdered in the East Indies. Like Columbus, he was trying to reach the East by sailing west, and this took him through the Straits of Magellan at the southern tip of South America.

Hernán Cortés (1485–1547, Spanish): did for the Aztecs in Mexico (whose emperor was Montezuma) much the same as Pizarro had done in Peru.

Francis Drake (1540–96, English): best known of the Elizabethan seafarers who were in constant battle with the Spaniards over control of the Caribbean (the Spanish Main) and its riches. Drake—in a ship called the *Pelican,* later renamed the *Golden Hind*—was the first Englishman to sail around the world. He was also pivotal in the English defeat of the Spanish Armada.

James Cook (1728–79, British): one of the great navigators of all time, made three expeditions to the Pacific in an attempt to discover the supposed great southern continent. He became the first European to land in New Zealand and also charted parts of Australia and Antarctica. His famous ships were the *Endeavour* and the *Resolution*. He is also remembered for devising a diet of limes—high in vitamin C, which protected his men against scurvy (the source of the nickname "limey" for the British). He was murdered in Hawaii.

Robert Falcon Scott (1868–1912, British): failed by a matter of days to become the first person to reach the South Pole, and died, with the rest of his party, in the course of the return journey. One of his companions was Captain Oates, who—knowing that his weakness was endangering the lives of the others—went out into the blizzard saying, "I may be some time."

Roald Amundsen (1872–1928, Norwegian): the one who made it to the South Pole—and back again. He was also the first to sail through the Northwest Passage, the sea route from Pacific to Atlantic along the north coast of North America.

GEOGRAPHY

"Geography is about maps," said E. Clerihew Bentley, and although geographers would take offense to that definition, a lot of what we learned as a kid was about the stuff that filled maps. The last section of this chapter should really be classed as paleontology, but nobody told us that at the time.

The Countries of the World

The world is divided into seven continents: Europe, Asia, North America, South America, Africa, Australia, and Antarctica. It's a matter of debate to which continent you assign various island nations, because a continent is by definition a continuous landmass. The islands of the Pacific are usually grouped together as Oceania, so for the purpose of this list, I am going to use that convention and place Australia under that heading, too. And I'm going to create a continent called Central America and include in it all the islands of the Caribbean, as well as the stretch of mainland south of Mexico.

Antarctica contains no countries—instead, it is a stateless territory protected from exploitation by an international treaty.

The countries listed here (with their capitals, continents, and any change of name since 1945) are the 192 members of the United Nations, the most recent being Montenegro, which split from Serbia in 2006; Switzerland, that long-term bastion of neutrality, finally succumbed in 2002. And they are given in the alphabetical order used by the United Nations, which provides such delights as The Former Yugoslav Republic of Macedonia, coming under T. SU or Y after a country's name means that it was formerly part of the Soviet Union or Yugoslavia.

Country	Capital	Continent
Afghanistan	Kabul	Asia
Albania	Tirana	Europe
Algeria	Algiers	Africa
Andorra	Andorra la Vella	Europe
Angola	Luanda	Africa
Antigua & Barbuda	St. John's	N. America
Argentina	Buenos Aires	S. America
Armenia (SU)	Yerevan	Asia
Australia	Canberra	Oceania
Austria	Vienna	Europe
Azerbaijan (SU)	Baku	Asia
Bahamas	Nassau	C. America
Bahrain	Manama	Asia
Bangladesh *formerly East Pakistan*	Dhaka	Asia
Barbados	Bridgetown	C. America
Belarus (SU)	Minsk	Europe
Belgium	Brussels	Europe
Belize	Belmopan	C. America
Benin *formerly Dahomey*	Porto Novo	Africa
Bhutan	Thimphu	Asia
Bolivia	La Paz	S. America

Country	Capital	Continent
Bosnia & Herzegovina (Y)	Sarajevo	Europe
Botswana *formerly Bechuanaland*	Gaborone	Africa
Brazil	Brasilia	S. America
Brunei Darussalam	Bandar Seri Begawan	Asia
Bulgaria	Sofia	Europe
Burkina Faso *formerly Upper Volta*	Ouagadougou	Africa
Burundi *formerly joined with Rwanda to form Ruanda-Urundi*	Bujumbura	Africa
Cambodia *known as Kampuchea from 1976–89*	Phnom Penh	Asia
Cameroon	Yaoundé	Africa
Canada	Ottawa	N. America
Cape Verde	Praia	Africa
Central African Republic	Bangui	Africa
Chad	N'Djamena	Africa
Chile	Santiago	S. America
China	Beijing	Asia
Colombia	Bogota	S. America
Comoros	Moroni	Africa
Congo, Republic of the *formerly the French Congo*	Brazzaville	Africa
Costa Rica	San José	C. America
Côte d'Ivoire *formerly the Ivory Coast*	Yamoussoukro	Africa
Croatia (Y)	Zagreb	Europe
Cuba	Havana	C. America
Cyprus	Nicosia	Europe

Country	Capital	Continent
Czech Republic *used to be joined to Slovakia to* *form Czechoslovakia*	Prague	Europe
Democratic People's Republic of Korea *(North Korea to you and me)*	Pyongyang	Asia
Democratic Republic of the Congo	Kinshasa	Africa
Denmark	Copenhagen	Europe
Djibouti *formerly the French Territory of* *the Afars and the Issas*	Djibouti City	Africa
Dominica	Roseau	C. America
Dominican Republic*	Santo Domingo	C. America
Ecuador	Quito	S. America
Egypt	Cairo	Africa
El Salvador	San Salvador	C. America
Equatorial Guinea	Malabo	Africa
Eritrea *gained independence from* *Ethiopia in 1993*	Asmara	Africa
Estonia (SU)	Tallinn	Europe
Ethiopia	Addis Ababa	Africa
Fiji	Suva	Oceania
Finland	Helsinki	Europe
France	Paris	Europe
Gabon	Libreville	Africa
Gambia	Banjul	Africa
Georgia (SU)	Tbilisi	Asia

* Easily confused: Dominica is one of the Lesser Antilles islands in the southeastern Caribbean; the Dominican Republic, farther north but still in the Caribbean, shares the island of Hispaniola with Haiti and forms part of the Greater Antilles.

Country	Capital	Continent
Germany *from 1949-90 was divided into West (Federal Republic) and east (Democratic Republic) with capitals Bonn and Berlin respectively*	Berlin	Europe
Ghana	Accra	Africa
Greece	Athens	Europe
Grenada	St. George's	C. America
Guatemala	Guatemala City	C. America
Guinea *formerly French Guinea*	Conakry	Africa
Guinea-Bissau** *formerly Portuguese Guinea*	Bissau	Africa
Guyana *formerly British Guiana*	Georgetown	S. America
Haiti	Port-au-Prince	C. America
Honduras	Tegucigalpa	C. America
Hungary	Budapest	Europe
Iceland	Reykjavik	Europe
India	New Delhi	Asia
Indonesia	Djakarta	Asia
Iran	Tehran	Asia
Iraq	Baghdad	Asia
Ireland	Dublin	Europe
Israel *created in 1948 in an area previously called Palestine*	Jerusalem	Asia
Italy	Rome	Europe
Jamaica	Kingston	C. America

** Guinea-Bissau and Guinea are next to each other on the Atlantic coast
of West Africa, frequently causing confusion.

Country	Capital	Continent
Japan	Tokyo	Asia
Jordan	Amman	Asia
Kazakhstan (SU)	Astana	Asia
Kenya	Nairobi	Africa
Kiribati *formerly Gilbert Islands*	Tarawa	Oceania
Kuwait	Kuwait City	Asia
Kyrgyzstan (SU)	Bishkek	Asia
Laos	Vientiane	Asia
Latvia (SU)	Riga	Europe
Lebanon	Beirut	Asia
Lesotho *formerly Basutoland*	Maseru	Africa
Liberia	Monrovia	Africa
Libya	Tripoli	Africa
Liechtenstein	Vaduz	Europe
Lithuania (SU)	Vilnius	Europe
Luxembourg	Luxembourg City	Europe
Madagascar	Antananarivo	Africa
Malawi *formerly Nyasaland*	Lilongwe	Africa
Malaysia *created in 1963 from the* *Federation of Malaya, the* *states of Sarawak and Sabah in* *Borneo, and briefly, Singapore*	Kuala Lumpur	Asia
Maldives	Malé	Asia
Mali	Bamako	Africa
Malta	Valletta	Europe
Marshall Islands	Delap-Uliga-Darrit	Oceania
Mauritania	Nouakchott	Africa

Country	Capital	Continent
Mauritius	Port Louis	Africa
Mexico	Mexico City	N. America
Micronesia, Federated States of	Palikir	Oceania
Moldova (SU)	Chisinau	Europe
Monaco	Monaco	Europe
Mongolia	Ulan Bator	Asia
Montenegro (Y)	Podgorica	Europe
Morocco	Rabat	Africa
Mozambique	Maputo	Africa
Myanmar *formerly Burma; the capital until 2006 was Rangoon/Yangon*	Nay Pyi Daw	Asia
Namibia *formerly South West Africa*	Windhoek	Africa
Nauru *formerly Pleasant Island*	Yaren	Oceania
Nepal	Kathmandu	Asia
Netherlands	Amsterdam	Europe
New Zealand	Wellington	Oceania
Nicaragua	Managua	C. America
Niger	Niamey	Africa
Nigeria	Abuja	Africa
Norway	Oslo	Europe
Oman	Muscat	Asia
Pakistan	Islamabad	Asia
Palau *formerly Belau*	Koror	Oceania
Panama	Panama City	C. America
Papua New Guinea	Port Moresby	Oceania

Country	Capital	Continent
Paraguay	Asunción	S. America
Peru	Lima	S. America
Philippines	Manila	Asia
Poland	Warsaw	Europe
Portugal	Lisbon	Europe
Qatar	Doha	Asia
Republic of Korea *(the South)*	Seoul	Asia
Romania	Bucharest	Europe
Russian Federation (SU)	Moscow	Europe/Asia
Rwanda *formerly joined with Burundi to form Ruanda-Urundi*	Kigali	Africa
Saint Kitts & Nevis	Basseterre	C. America
Saint Lucia	Castries	C. America
Saint Vincent & the Grenadines	Kingstown	C. America
Samoa	Apia & Pago Pago	Oceania
San Marino	San Marino	Europe
São Tomé & Príncipe	São Tomé	Africa
Saudi Arabia	Riyadh	Asia
Senegal	Dakar	Africa
Serbia (Y)	Belgrade	Europe
Seychelles	Victoria	Africa
Sierra Leone	Freetown	Africa
Singapore *became independent of the Malaysian Federation in 1965*	Singapore	Asia

Country	Capital	Continent
Slovakia *used to be joined to the Czech* *Republic to form Czechoslovakia*	Bratislava	Europe
Slovenia (Y)	Ljubljana	Europe
Solomon Islands	Honiara	Oceania
Somalia	Mogadishu	Africa
South Africa	Pretoria	Africa
Spain	Madrid	Europe
Sri Lanka *formerly Ceylon*	Colombo	Asia
Sudan	Khartoum	Africa
Suriname *formerly Dutch Guiana*	Paramaribo	S. America
Swaziland	Mbabane	Africa
Sweden	Stockholm	Europe
Switzerland	Berne	Europe
Syria	Damascus	Asia
Tajikistan (SU)	Dushanbe	Asia
Thailand	Bangkok	Asia
The Former Yugoslav Republic of Macedonia	Skopje	Europe
Timor-Leste (East Timor)	Dili	Asia
Togo	Lomé	Africa
Tonga	Nuku'alofa	Oceania
Trinidad & Tobago	Port-of-Spain	C. America
Tunisia	Tunis	Africa
Turkey	Ankara	Europe/Asia
Turkmenistan (SU)	Ashgabat	Asia
Tuvalu *formerly Ellice Islands*	Funafuti	Oceania

Country	Capital	Continent
Uganda	Kampala	Africa
Ukraine (SU)	Kiev	Europe
United Arab Emirates	Abu Dhabi	Asia
United Kingdom of Great Britain & Northern Ireland	London	Europe
United Republic of Tanzania *formed in 1964 from a union of Tanganyika and Zanzibar*	Dodoma	Africa
United States of America	Washington	N. America
Uruguay	Montevideo	S. America
Uzbekistan (SU)	Tashkent	Asia
Vanuatu *formerly New Hebrides*	Port Vila	Oceania
Venezuela	Caracas	S. America
Vietnam *from 1954–76 divided into North and South, with Hanoi the capital of the North and Saigon (now Ho Chi Minh City) of the South*	Hanoi	Asia
Yemen	San'a	Asia
Zambia *formerly Northern Rhodesia*	Lusaka	Africa
Zimbabwe *formerly Southern Rhodesia, then from 1964–79 Rhodesia; until 1979 the capital was called Salisbury*	Harare	Africa

The 50 United States of America

Listed below are the 50 states with their nicknames, their capitals, and the date they entered the Union. Those marked with an asterisk are the original 13 colonies that declared themselves independent from British rule in 1776. Those marked with two asterisks seceded from the Union during the Civil War and formed the Confederate States of America; all had been readmitted by 1870.

State	Nickname	Capital	Date
Alabama **	Yellowhammer State	Montgomery	1819
Alaska	The Last Frontier	Juneau	1959
Arizona	Grand Canyon State	Phoenix	1912
Arkansas **	Natural State	Little Rock	1836
California	Golden State	Sacramento	1850
Colorado	Centennial State	Denver	1876
Connecticut *	Constitution State	Hartford	1788
Delaware*	First State	Dover	1787
Florida **	Sunshine State	Tallahassee	1845
Georgia * **	Peach State	Atlanta	1788
Hawaii	Aloha State	Honolulu	1959
Idaho	Gem State	Boise	1890
Illinois	Prairie State	Springfield	1818
Indiana	Hoosier State	Indianapolis	1816

State	Nickname	Capital	Date
Iowa	Hawkeye State	Des Moines	1846
Kansas	Sunflower State	Topeka	1861
Kentucky	Bluegrass State	Frankfort	1792
Louisiana **	Pelican State	Baton Rouge	1812
Maine	Pine Tree State	Augusta	1820
Maryland *	Old Line State	Annapolis	1788
Massachusetts *	Bay State	Boston	1788
Michigan	Great Lakes State	Lansing	1837
Minnesota	North Star State	St. Paul	1858
Mississippi **	Magnolia State	Jackson	1817
Missouri	Show-me State	Jefferson City	1821
Montana	Treasure State	Helena	1889
Nebraska	Cornhusker State	Lincoln	1867
Nevada	Silver State	Carson City	1864
New Hampshire *	Granite State	Concord	1788
New Jersey *	Garden State	Trenton	1787
New Mexico	Land of Enchantment	Santa Fe	1912
New York *	Empire State	Albany	1788
N. Carolina * **	Tar Heel State	Raleigh	1789
North Dakota	Peace Garden State	Bismarck	1889
Ohio	Buckeye State	Columbus	1803
Oklahoma	Sooner State	Oklahoma City	1907
Oregon	Beaver State	Salem	1859
Pennsylvania *	Keystone State	Harrisburg	1787

State	Nickname	Capital	Date
Rhode Island *	Ocean State	Providence	1790
S. Carolina * **	Palmetto State	Columbia	1788
South Dakota	Mount Rushmore State	Pierre	1889
Tennessee **	Volunteer State	Nashville	1796
Texas **	Lone Star State	Austin	1845
Utah	Beehive State	Salt Lake City	1896
Vermont	Green Mountain State	Montpelier	1791
Virginia * **	The Old Dominion	Richmond	1788
Washington	Evergreen State	Olympia	1889
West Virginia	Mountain State	Charleston	1863
Wisconsin	Badger State	Madison	1848
Wyoming	Equality State	Cheyenne	1890

The District of Columbia is a federal district, not a state, sharing its boundaries with the city of Washington, D.C.

The Canadian Provinces and its Territories

In 1867 Canada became a self-governing dominion. The country is made up of seven provinces and three territories, the difference being that the provinces receive their power from the Monarchy, and the territories from the federal government. The territories are marked with an asterisk.

Province	Nickname	Capitol	Year
Alberta	The Princess Province	Edmonton	1905

Province	Nickname	Capitol	Year
British Columbia	The Pacific Province	Victoria	1871
Manitoba	The Keystone Province	Winnipeg	1870
New Brunswick	The Loyalist Province	Fredericton	1867
Newfoundland and Labrador	The Rock	St. John's	1949
Northwest Territories*		Yellowknife	1870
Nova Scotia	Canada's Ocean Playground	Halifax	1867
Nunavit*		Iquluit	1999
Ontario		Toronto	1867
Prince Edward Island	The Garden Province	Charlottetown	1873
Quebec	The Beautiful Province	Quebec	1867
Saskatchewan	The Wheat Province	Regina	1905
Yukon*	Land of the Midnight Sun	Whitehorse	1898

The World's Highest Mountains

All the mountains in the world that top 26,244 feet (8,000 m) are in the Himalayas, which is frankly a bit boring for a book like this, but what can you do?

Mountain	Country	Feet	Meters
Everest	China/Nepal	29,029	8,848

Mountain	Country	Feet	Meters
K2 (Godley Austen)	China/Kashmir	28,251	8,611
Kanchenjunga	India/Nepal	28,209	8,598
Lhotse	China/Nepal	27,940	8,516
Makalu	China/Nepal	27,825	8,481
Cho Oyu	China/Nepal	26,906	8,201
Dhaulagiri	Nepal	26,811	8,172
Manaslu	Nepal	26,759	8,156
Nanga Parbut	Kashmir	26,660	8,126
Annapurna	Nepal	26,503	8,078
Gasherbrum	China/Kashmir	26,470	8,068
Broad Peak	China/Kashmir	26,414	8,051
Xixabangma	China	26,286	8,012

There are another 20 that are above 22,966 feet (7,000 m), all still in Asia; then we shift to South America for Aconagua in Argentina, which is 22,835 feet (6,960 m).

And 19 more above 20,341 feet (6,200 m), all in the Andes, before it is worth even glancing elsewhere.

Here is a list of the top three from the other continents:

Mountain	Country	Feet	Meters
NORTH AMERICA			
McKinley	U.S. (Alaska)	20,322	6,194

Mountain	Country	Feet	Meters
Logan	U.S.	19,551	5,959
Citlaltepetl	Mexico	18,701	5,700
AFRICA			
Kilimanjaro	Tanzania	19,341	5,895
Mount Kenya	Kenya	17,057	5,199
Ruwenzori	Uganda/Zaire	16,762	5,109
ANTARCTICA			
Vinson Massif		16,066	4,897
Mount Kirkpatrick		14,856	4,528
Mount Markham		14,268	4,349
EUROPE			
Mont Blanc	France/Italy	15,771	4,807
Monte Rosa	Italy/Switzerland	15,203	4,634
Dom	Switzerland	14,911	4,545
OCEANIA			
Mount Wilhelm	Papua New Guinea	14,790	4,508
Aoraki *(formerly Mount Cook)*	New Zealand	12,313	3,753
Mount Balbi	Solomon Islands	8,002	2,439

The World's Largest Bodies of Water

The four principal oceans of the world with areas in square miles (sq km) are:

OCEANS

Ocean	Square miles	Sq km
Pacific	69,374	179,679
Atlantic	35,665	92,373
Indian	28,539	73,917
Arctic	5,440	14,090

SEAS

Sea	Location	Square miles	Sq km
South China	between mainland Asia & the Philippines	1,149	2,975
Caribbean	east of Central America	1,068	2,766
Mediter-ranean	between Europe and Africa	971	2,516
Bering	at the very north of the Pacific, between Alaska and Russia	875	2,268
Gulf of Mexico	south of the eastern U.S., east of Mexico	596	1,543
Sea of Okhotsk	south of eastern Russia, north of Japan	590	1,528

Sea	Location	Square miles	Sq km
East China & Yellow	east of mainland China, north of South China, and south of the Okhotsk	482	1,249
Hudson Bay	Canada	475	1,232
Sea of Japan	between Japan and eastern Asia	389	1,008
North	east of the UK, bounded on the east by Denmark	222	575

The deepest point in the world is the Mariana Trench (in the Pacific, east of the Philippines), at 36,161 feet (11,022 m).

The World's Longest Rivers

The world's longest rivers are more fairly divided than its mountains, so here are the 17 that are longer than 2,175 miles (3,500 km), with the countries they mostly flow through:

River	Location	Miles	Km
Nile	Egypt	4,145	6,670
Amazon	Brazil	4,008	6,450
Yangtze	China	3,964	6,380
Mississippi–Missouri	U.S.	3,748	6,020
Yenisey–Angara	Russia	3,448	5,550
Huang He	China	3,395	5,464
Ob–Irtysh	Russia	3,361	5,410

River	Location	Miles	Km
Zaire/Congo	Zaire/Congo	2,901	4,670
Mekong	Vietnam/Cambodia	2,796	4,500
Paraná–Plate	Argentina	2,796	4,500
Amur	Russia	2,734	4,400
Lena	Russia	2,734	4,400
Mackenzie	Canada	2,634	4,240
Niger	Nigeria/Niger/Mali	2,597	4,180
Murray–Darling	Australia	2,330	3,750
Volga	Russia	2,299	3,700
Zambezi	Mozambique/ Zimbabwe/Zambia	2,199	3,540

If you counted the Mississippi and Missouri as two separate rivers, they would both still find a place on this list, as would the Ob and Irtysh. The Yenisey on its own would also qualify.

Geological Time

The largest subdivision of geological time is an **era**, which can be divided into **periods** and then into **epochs**. The major divisions tend to be marked by mass extinctions, with smaller ones indicated by smaller extinctions and/or climate change. There have been three main eras; anything earlier than this was referred to as Precambrian.

☞ PALEOZOIC ERA, FROM ABOUT 600–250 MYA (MILLION YEARS AGO)

Paleozoic literally means *ancient life*. Life on Earth had existed for perhaps 4,000 million years before this, but it consisted largely of single-celled creatures such as algae and bacteria. The Cambrian period, the first part of the Paleozoic, is when bigger creatures—some of them with backbones—began to emerge, although they were still living in the sea. The Paleozoic was followed by the Permian extinction, when 95 percent of all life on Earth—plants and animals on both land and sea—died. Just like that. Just when they were beginning to get the hang of it. (To be fair, the period of extinction lasted millions of years, so "just like that" is an exaggeration, but scientists still don't know for sure why it happened.)

Anyway, it paved the way for…

☞ MESOZOIC ERA, FROM ABOUT 250–65 MYA

Mesozoic means *middle life*. This was the age of the dinosaurs, and it was divided into three periods:

- **Triassic** (*c.* 250–220 mya): the time of the first dinosaurs, small and agile to start with but poised to take over the world.
- **Jurassic** (*c.* 220–155 mya): when giant herbivores such as *Apatosaurus* (which used to be called Brontosaurus) and *Diplodocus* ruled.
- **Cretaceous** (*c.* 150–65 mya): dominated by *Tyrannosaurus rex*, but also the time when plants first produced flowers.

Then along came the Cretaceous–Tertiary (known as the KT) extinction, when the Earth may or may not have been hit by a meteorite. Nothing quite as bad as the Permian but still enough to wipe out the dinosaurs, and following that…

☞ CENOZOIC ERA, FROM ABOUT 65 MYA TO THE PRESENT

Cenozoic means *recent life*. This is when mammals and birds took over. It is sometimes divided into the Tertiary and Quaternary periods and then subdivided into these epochs:

- **Palaeocene** (65–55 mya): when the first large mammals emerged to fill the gaps left by the dinosaurs.
- **Eocene** (55–35 mya): a period of great warmth, when the first grasses started to grow.
- **Oligocene** (35–25 mya): when mammals and flowering plants began to greatly diversify.
- **Miocene** (25–5.5 mya): when the common ancestor of human beings and primates emerged.
- **Pliocene** (5.5–2 mya): when that same common ancestor came down from the trees.
- **Pleistocene** (2 million–11,750 years ago—this is where you enter the Quaternary period if you belong to that school of thought.): mammoths and Neanderthal man came and went, but *Homo sapiens* may be here to stay.
- **Holocene** (11,750 years ago–present, but see below): the emergence of agriculture and thus of the first civilizations.

There is a suggestion that the Holocene period finished in the year 1800 and that human impact since the time of the Industrial Revolution justifies us designating a new period, the Anthropocene.

GENERAL STUDIES

This chapter covers various subjects that didn't fit elsewhere in the book: mythology, art, music—all the subjects that weren't included in the exams but you had to learn a bit of anyway.

World Religions

There are, of course, lots of them and lots of subdivisions within them, but here is a little about the five really big ones, starting with the oldest.

☞ JUDAISM

Monotheistic religion whose beginnings are lost in the mists of time. Its adherents are called Jews, their god is eternal and invisible, and trusting in God's will is a fundamental tenet. Jewish law as revealed by God is contained in the Torah, which comprises the first five books of the Christian Old Testament. The Wailing Wall in Jerusalem is a sacred site.

☞ HINDUISM

Polytheistic, about 5,000 years old, and followed primarily in India. One of its tenets is that one's actions lead to the reward or punishment of being reincarnated in a higher or lower form of life. The aim is to be freed from this cycle and attain the state of unchanging reality known as Brahman. The three principal creator gods are Brahma, Vishnu, and Shiva, but

Krishna (an incarnation of Vishnu) is also widely worshipped. The main scriptures are the Vedas. The Ganges River is seen as a goddess of purity and pilgrims come to the holy city of Varanesi (Benares) to bathe in the river. The cow is a sacred symbol of fertility.

☞ BUDDHISM

Founded in the 6th century B.C. by Gautama Siddhartha, known as the Buddha or "Awakened One." There are no gods in Buddhism; its adherents follow the philosophy expressed in the Buddha's Four Noble Truths—that existence is characterized by suffering, that suffering is caused by desire, that to end desire is therefore to end suffering, and that this may be achieved by following the Eightfold Path to the ideal state of nirvana.

☞ CHRISTIANITY

Monotheistic religion that grew out of Judaism 2,000 years ago and is based on the belief that Jesus Christ is the son of God. The holy book is the Bible, divided into the Old and New testaments; the New Testament is the one concerned with the teachings of Christ and his apostles. The church divided initially into Eastern (Orthodox) and Western (Roman Catholic) branches. The Catholic Church still recognizes the Pope as leader and Rome as a holy city, but a major rift beginning in the 16th century led to the emergence of the Protestants and many subsequent subdivisions. Jerusalem is the traditional site of Christ's burial and resurrection.

☞ ISLAM

Monotheistic religion whose god is called Allah, founded in the 7th century A.D. by the one prophet, Mohammed. The holy book—the Koran or Qur'an—contains the revelations that Allah made to Mohammed. The holy cities are Mecca, birthplace of Mohammed, and Medina, where he is buried. All able-bodied Muslims who can afford it are expected to make a pilgrimage (*hadj*) to Medina at least once in their lives. The Dome of the Rock in Jerusalem is the oldest intact Muslim temple in the world and is built over the point from which Mohammed traditionally ascended to heaven.

☞ THE TEN COMMANDMENTS

Given to Moses by God on Mount Sinai (remember Charlton Heston and those massive tablets?), these are a basic code of conduct for both Jews and Christians.

1. Thou shalt have no other gods before me.
2. Thou shalt not make unto thee any graven image, or any likeness of any thing that is in heaven above or that is in the earth beneath, or that is in the water under the earth.
3. Thou shalt not take the name of the Lord thy God in vain.
4. Remember the Sabbath day and keep it holy.
5. Honor thy father and thy mother.
6. Thou shalt not kill.
7. Thou shalt not commit adultery.
8. Thou shalt not steal.
9. Thou shalt not bear false witness against thy neighbor.
10. Thou shalt not covet thy neighbor's house, thou shalt not covet thy neighbor's wife, nor his manservant, nor his maidservant, nor his ox, nor his ass, nor any thing that is thy neighbor's.

Roman Numerals

I =	1	C =	100
V =	5	D =	500
X =	10	M =	1,000
L =	50		

From there, the Romans could make up any number they wanted—except, interestingly enough, zero, because they didn't have a symbol for it. They made the other numbers by adding (putting letters at the end) or subtracting (putting them at the beginning).

For example:

$$I = 1$$
$$II = 2$$
III = 3   but IV (for example, 1 before 5) = 4

Similarly,

$$V = 5$$
$$VI = 6$$
$$VII = 7$$
VIII = 8   but IX (1 before 10) = 9

The same principle applies with the big numbers, so you end up with something like XLIV (44, because it is 10 before 50 and 1 before 5) and CDXCIX (499, made up of 100 before 500, 10 before 100, and 1 before 10). You would have thought 499 might be ID (1 before 500), but it isn't.

The Seven Wonders of the World

The Seven Wonders of the Ancient World, described in an old encyclopedia as "remarkable for their splendor or magnitude," were:

- The Hanging Gardens of Babylon
- The Mausoleum at Halicarnassus
- The Lighthouse of Alexandria
- The Colossus of Rhodes
- The Temple of Artemis at Ephesus
- The Statue of Zeus at Olympia
- The Great Pyramid of Giza

Of the seven, only the Great Pyramid is still in existence.

A Bit of Classical Mythology

There are lots of Greek and Roman gods, as well as enough mythological characters and demigods to fill a book on their own, but these are some you might remember:

Greek Name	Roman Equivalent	God of…
Zeus	Jupiter	father of the gods, also god of thunder
Hera	Juno	his wife and sister, goddess of marriage
Apollo	Apollo	god of hunting and of healing, who was consulted at the Oracle of Delphi
Ares	Mars	god of war
Aphrodite	Venus	goddess of love
Artemis	Diana	goddess of hunting and the moon

Greek Name	Roman Equivalent	God of…
Hermes	Mercury	messenger of the gods, who wore the winged sandals and helmet
Athena	Minerva	goddess of war and wisdom
Hephaestus	Vulcan	god of fire
Poseidon	Neptune	god of the sea
Demeter	Ceres	goddess of corn and the harvest
Dis	Pluto	god of the underworld

Famous Artists

This was meant to be a Top 20, but the list kept growing. There are so many artists that have contributed to the wonderful world of art we know today that I found I couldn't leave any of these names out.

Sandro Botticelli (1445–1510, Italian): best known for *The Birth of Venus* (Venus with flowing hair, standing in a shell).

Leonardo da Vinci (1452–1519, Italian): painter, sculptor, inventor, and all-around polymath—one of the great figures of the Renaissance. Among many of his celebrated works are *Mona Lisa* and *The Last Supper*.

Michelangelo Buonarotti (1475–1564, Italian): painter—most famous for the ceiling of the Sistine Chapel in the Vatican—and sculptor of the statue of *David* in Florence.

Raphael (1483–1520, Italian): painter of many versions of the Madonna and Child; and of frescoes, notably *The School of Athens* for the Sistine Chapel.

Titian (*c*. 1490–1576, Italian): greatest painter of the Venetian school. His religious and mythological subjects include *Assumption of the Virgin* and *Bacchus and Ariadne*.

Hans Holbein the Younger (*c*. 1497–1543, German, latterly in England): court painter to Henry VIII, responsible for the flattering portrait of Anne of Cleves, which encouraged the king to marry her.

Pieter Brueghel the Elder (1525–69, Flemish): famous for scenes of peasant life and landscapes.

El Greco (Domenikos Theotokopoulos, 1541–1614, Greek living in Spain): used distinctive elongated figures in his paintings of saints and in *The Burial of Count Orgaz*.

Peter Paul Rubens (1577–1640, Flemish): greatest of the Baroque artists, based mainly in Antwerp. Painted the ceiling of the Banqueting Hall in Whitehall, London, but is best remembered for depictions of abundantly fleshy women.

Frans Hals (*c*. 1581–1666, Dutch): best known for portraiture. Painter of *The Laughing Cavalier*.

Diego de Velázquez (1599–1660, Spanish): court painter to Philip IV, producing many portraits of his patron and his family, notably *Las Meninas*. Also *The Rokeby Venus*, painted where the goddess is lying naked on a bed, facing away from the viewer, and looking at herself in a mirror.

Rembrandt van Rijn (1606–69, Dutch): prolific portraitist and self-portraitist; creator of *The Night Watch*, the most famous painting in the Rijksmuseum in Amsterdam.

Jan Vermeer (1632–75, Dutch): based in Delft and noted for his skillful use of light; painted everyday scenes of women reading or writing letters or playing musical instruments. Best known for his oil on canvas, *Girl with a Pearl Earring.*

Canaletto (Giovanni Canal, 1697–1768, Italian): famous for his views of Venice, but also spent time in London and painted scenes of the Thames.

William Hogarth (1697–1764, British): engraver; hard-hitting social satires such as *The Rake's Progress* and *Gin Lane.*

Francisco de Goya (1746–1828, Spanish): painter, notably of the portraits *Maja Clothed* and *Maja Nude,* and the dramatic *Shootings of May 3rd 1808,* inspired by Spanish resistance to French occupation.

J(ohn) M(allord) W(illiam) Turner (1775–1851, British): prolific painter of landscapes and maritime scenes, most famously *The Fighting Téméraire.* His use of color and light and his portrayal of weather inspired the French Impressionists Monet and Renoir.

John Constable (1776–1837, British): painter of landscapes, notably *The Haywain.*

Edouard Manet (1832–83, French): established before the Impressionists, he adopted some of their techniques but was never quite one of that school. Famous works include *Déjeuner sur l'Herbe* (the one where the men are fully dressed and the women are not) and *A Bar at the Folies-Bergère.*

James McNeill Whistler (1834–1903, American, working in England): painter, notably of *The Artist's Mother*; also known as a wit. When Oscar Wilde remarked, "How I wish I'd said that," Whistler responded, "You will, Oscar, you will."

Edgar Degas (1834–1917, French): Impressionist who painted all those ballet dancers.

Paul Cézanne (1839–1906, French): post-Impressionist and precursor of cubism, based in Provence. In addition to landscapes, famous works include *The Card Players* and various groups of women bathing.

Claude Monet (1840–1926, French): most important painter of the Impressionist movement, famous for the "series" paintings that studied the effect of light at different times of day and year on the same subject: Rouen cathedral, haystacks and poplars. Lived latterly at Giverny, outside Paris, now a much visited garden, and painted a series of the waterlilies (*nymphéas*) there.

Auguste Rodin (1840–1917, French): sculptor, most famously of *The Kiss*, *The Thinker*, and *The Burghers of Calais*.

Pierre-Auguste Renoir (1841–1919, French): Impressionist, best known for *Les Parapluies* and *Le Moulin de la Galette* (a bar in Montmartre).

Paul Gauguin (1848–1903, French): the one who went to Tahiti and painted the people there.

Vincent van Gogh (1853–90, Dutch, working mainly in France): cut off part of his ear and subsequently committed suicide. Self-portraits, *The Potato Eaters*, *Sunflowers*, *The Starry Night*.

John Singer Sargent (1856–1925, American): portrait painter of the stars, including Ellen Terry, John D. Rockefeller, and various young ladies of fashion.

Henri de Toulouse-Lautrec (1864–1901, French): the little one. Lived in Montmartre and painted music halls, cafés, and their habitués. Works include *At the Moulin Rouge* and *La Toilette*.

Pablo Picasso (1881–1973, Spanish, working mostly in France): arguably the greatest and certainly the most versatile painter of the 20th century. After the famous "rose" and "blue" periods of his early years, he was fundamental to the development of cubism, expanded the technique of collage, became involved with the surrealists, designed ballet costumes, and did a bit of pottery. His greatest painting is probably *Guernica*, a nightmarish portrayal of the horrors of the Spanish Civil War.

Salvador Dalí (1914–89, Spanish): surrealist and notable egomaniac. Studied abnormal psychology and dream symbolism and reproduced its imagery in his paintings. Also worked with the surrealist film director Luis Buñuel (*Le Chien Andalou*) and designed the dream sequence in Alfred Hitchcock's *Spellbound*. His painting of the Last Supper is the one that shows the arms and torso of Christ floating above the disciples at the table.

Jackson Pollock (1912–56, American): abstract expressionist painter who believed that the act of painting was more important than the finished product. His paintings are therefore highly colorful and chaotic to the point of frenzy. And often huge.

Famous Composers

I was much more disciplined with this list—my Top 20 actually has 20 people in it.

Antonio Vivaldi (1678–1741, Italian): composed operas and church music galore but is now mostly remembered for *The Four Seasons*, a suite of violin concertos.

Johann Sebastian Bach (1685–1750, German): highly esteemed and vastly influential composer—without him there might have been no Haydn, no Mozart, and no Beethoven. Wrote mostly organ music, church music, and orchestral music, such as the *Brandenburg Concertos*, the *St. Matthew Passion, The Well-Tempered Clavier,* and *Jesu Joy of Man's Desiring.* Came from a famous musical family and had many children, including the composers Carl Philip Emmanuel and Johann Christian; the latter moved to London and became known as the English Bach.

George Frideric Handel (1685–1759, German, working in England): successful in Germany before moving to England when George I became king; wrote the *Water Music* for him. Also wrote a number of operas and developed the English oratorio, of which *Messiah* (which contains the *Hallelujah Chorus*) is the best known; composed the anthem *Zadok the Priest* for the coronation of George II.

Franz Josef Haydn (1732–1809, Austrian): "Papa Haydn," another vastly prolific composer, credited with the development of the classical symphony (he wrote 104 of them, including the *London* and the *Clock*) and the four-movement string quartet.

Wolfgang Amadeus Mozart (1756–91, Austrian): infant prodigy and all-around genius. Composer of 41 symphonies, including the *Jupiter;* operas, including *Don Giovanni* and *The Magic Flute*; innumerable concertos, sonatas, solo piano pieces, and chamber music. Not bad for someone who died at 35.

Ludwig van Beethoven (1770–1827, German): wrote nine symphonies, but the ones we all know are the Fifth (da-da-da-DAH) and the Ninth (the *Choral Symphony*, whose last movement includes the glorious *Song of Joy*—amazing to think that he was already deaf by this time and never heard it performed). Also wrote *Für Elise*, a piano piece studied laboriously by generations of budding pianists. And lots of other stuff, including one opera, called *Fidelio*.

Gioachino Rossini (1792–1868, Italian): known mostly for operas, including *La Cenerentola, The Barber of Seville,* and *William Tell,* which boasts the world's most famous overture.

Franz Schubert (1797–1828, Austrian): wrote about 600 songs (*lieder*) and *The Trout* piano quintet. This ambitious career seems odd, then, that he would ever leave anything unfinished. But when we talk about the *Unfinished Symphony,* we tend to mean Schubert's Eighth.

Frédéric Chopin (1810–49, Polish): wrote some beautiful tear-jerking stuff for the piano, much of it influenced by Polish folk music: mazurkas, polonaises, waltzes, and short romantic pieces called nocturnes, a term he popularized.

Franz Liszt (1811–86, Hungarian): virtuoso pianist, possibly the best there has ever been, as well as a prolific composer. His best-known works are probably the *Hungarian Rhapsodies*. His daughter Cosima became Mrs. Richard Wagner.

Richard Wagner (1813–83, German): was once said that he had wonderful moments but bad quarters of an hour. Fans of his work use words like "a masterpiece" and "greatest achieve-ment in the history of opera," but given that the four "musical dramas" that comprise the *Ring* cycle run for a total of nearly 16 hours, I am never going to find out firsthand.

Giuseppe Verdi (1813–1901, Italian): wrote rather shorter operas, notably *Rigoletto, La Traviata, Don Carlos,* and *Aida*.

Pyotr Tchaikovsky (1840–93, Russian): best known as a composer of ballet music (*The Nutcracker Suite, Swan Lake,*

The Sleeping Beauty) but also wrote the wonderfully loud and patriotic *1812 Overture* after Napoleon had been forced to retreat from Moscow.

Edward Elgar (1857–1934, English): responsible for the *Enigma Variations*, including *Pomp and Circumstance* ("Land of Hope and Glory").

Giacomo Puccini (1858–1924, Italian): another one for the opera buffs—*La Bohème, Tosca, Madama Butterfly, Turandot.* My reference book says he "lacks the nobility of Verdi" but makes up for it in dramatic flair and skill. And he certainly wrote tunes.

Arnold Schoenberg (1874–1951, Austrian): wrote only a few tunes but invented a form of music called atonality and, later, serialism, which are bywords for "unlistenable" to many people.

Gustav Mahler (1860–1911, Austrian): became widely known after Tom Lehrer wrote a song about his wife, Alma, but he was also a great conductor and wrote some good music, too. This included nine finished symphonies and an unfinished one, all on a grand scale, and a song-symphony called *Das Lied von der Erde* ("The Song of the Earth").

Gustav Holst (1874–1934, English): best known for the *Planets* suite, which has seven parts—Earth was not deemed worthy of inclusion and Pluto was not discovered yet. Which is convenient in light of recent events.

Igor Stravinsky (1882–1971, Russian): composed the *Firebird Suite* specifically for Diaghilev's Ballets Russes and followed this with *Petrushka* and *The Rite of Spring.* His style was always experimental, and he turned to neoclassicism and later to serialism, but he was never in the same league as Schoenberg for making people reach for the "off" button.

Sergei Prokofiev (1891–1953, Russian): included because of *Peter and the Wolf*, a symphonic fairy tale that I listened to at school and that crops up on TV every so often. *The Oxford Dictionary of Music* says that it is "delightful in itself and a wonderful way of instructing children (and others) how to identify orchestral instruments." Oh, and he wrote other things, too, starting when he was about three: symphonies, ballets (*Romeo and Juliet, Cinderella*), operas, film music (*Alexander Nevsky*), and more.

The Planets

When I was at school, learning the planets was pretty straightforward. There were nine planets in our solar system. Starting at the Sun and working outward, we learned of Mercury, Venus, Earth, Mars, Jupiter, Saturn, Uranus, Neptune, and Pluto. And there were sundry mnemonics to help you remember, along the lines of My Very Educated Mother Just Served Us Nine Pizzas.

Then they began making new discoveries. Most important, in 2003, they discovered an icy body that was larger than Pluto, which brought the whole definition of a planet into question. After much controversy a conference of the International Astronomical Union in 2006 deemed that Pluto no longer qualified. The icy body became known as Eris—after the Greek goddess of discord, which was very appropo, given all the trouble she had caused.

So there are now officially eight major planets—the first eight on the original list—with Pluto and Eris demoted to the status of minor planets or ice dwarfs.

Enjoy These Other Reader's Digest Best-Sellers

Featuring all the memory-jogging tips you'll ever need to know, this fun little book will help you recall hundreds of important facts using simple, easy-to-remember mnemonics from your school days.

$14.95 hardcover
ISBN 978–0–7621–0917–3

Fun and interesting facts and quips about authors and books sure to delight the bibliophile and make anyone the life of the literary party. Covering both modern and classic literature—and those popular guilty pleasures—this book will interest both bookworms and trivia buffs.

$14.95 hardcover
ISBN 978-1-60652-034-5

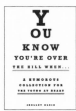

This laugh-out-loud collection of heartwarming jokes, quips, and truisms about the joys of aging will keep you entertained for hours.

$14.95 hardcover
ISBN 978–1–60652–025–3

Confused about when to use "its" or "it's" or the correct spelling of "principal" or "principle"? Avoid language pitfalls and let this entertaining and practical guide improve both your speaking and writing skills.

$14.95 hardcover
ISBN 978–1–60652–026–0

Do you know who really designed and sewed the first flag? It wasn't Betsy Ross! The answer to this and hundreds of other fascinating myth-debunking facts of U.S. history will delight history buffs and trivia lovers alike.

$14.95 hardcover
ISBN 978–1–60652–035–2

Reader's Digest books can be purchased through retail and online bookstores.
In the United States books are distributed by Penguin Group (USA), Inc.
For more information or to order books, call 1-800-788-6262.